ENERGY INTELLIGENCE AT WORK

BY CLAIRE CHIDLEY

Gatehouse Press
The Gatehouse
1 Pigeons Farm Road
Greenham
Berkshire
RG19 8XG

Ordering Information:
Quantity sales. Special discounts are available on quantity purchases by corporations, associations, and others. For details, contact the address above.

Energy Intelligence at Work by Claire Chidley—1st ed.
ISBN 978-0-9569724-3-9

ACKNOWLEDGEMENTS

*'Thanks to Julie, Robin Mansfield and Helen Bennett.
I couldn't have done this without your help'.*

Contents

PREFACE

A Chief Executive in a local authority once told me that when he was promoted to his current role, he spent his first day in work meeting his staff. Having listened to people all day, he returned to his office tired but excited about the job and the challenges and opportunities that lay ahead. He said; "I sat at my big plush desk and reflected for a moment on how far I'd come. I was daunted about what to do next, where to start. Then I knew there was one essential phone call I needed to make that would really help me. I picked up the phone and rang.....my mother!"

When I was promoted into a senior management position, I too went through similar feelings and I remembered the Chief Executive's story. After a few days of getting to grips with my new role, I too rang my mum and invited her to visit my workplace and have lunch afterwards.

We walked around the building and the grounds on a lovely summer's day chatting to people in the different departments. My mum at the time was 75, a little hard of hearing and not as fit as she once was. She did very well on my 'grand tour', meeting staff and visiting their offices.

Later, when we were sitting in a local cafe with a sandwich and coffee, she gave me her view and it was a surprising one. She said: "It's a lovely space and the people are nice, but it isn't buzzing is it? It's like the living dead in there. You're going to have to do something to liven up the place, to energise people and get them going." She smiled and bit into her sandwich.

She was right. There was something missing, a magic ingredient that would lift the organisation from being 'fair to middling' to 'good' and it was related to *the energy of the place and its people.*

If I were being honest, I'd already observed many people 'cruising in neutral', carrying out their tasks in a routine way without a care for the impact they were having on colleagues and the ultimate effect on their customers. People seemed exhausted and depleted by their workload without any means of coming off the pace to re-charge. They seemed disinterested, bored and unchallenged by what they were doing. The sum total of all this was a confusing environment of frenetic energy full of shoddy mistakes and poor quality services because too many corners were being cut or an apathetic response that missed deadlines and customer expectations by a mile.

Could the workforce be helped to be lively and full of get-up-and-go? What could be done to put some 'oomph' into everything, to make people excited and fired-up about their work? Could I somehow play a part in putting some positive energy into the place and keep it at a measured flow to avoid the extremes I was witnessing?

I realised that my mother had highlighted something I already knew without consciously being aware of it. Every time I entered a workplace regardless of whatever sector or type of business they were in, I had an immediate sense of their energy levels and that seemed linked somehow to their success.

Some places had a real buzz to them. People seemed focused, happy and committed and high performing. Others had some parts that were energised and some that were not, and a few were drained, de-motivated, confused and lacklustre.

These experiences had informed an impression and I decided to give it more thought. If I could capture the essence of this energy, how it worked and what people could do to maintain optimum energy for their workplace, the benefits could be great not just for their own working environment, but perhaps more widely in society.

I had no idea how to proceed until a train journey, a book and Albert Einstein gave me my 'eureka' moment a few months later. In the meantime, I made a commitment to trying to understand what I now call 'Energy Intelligence'. This book explains my breakthrough to developing the 'intelligence', the theory and its practical applications so that you, in whatever role you have in work can raise your energy levels to improve your performance, personal satisfaction and success for yourself and those around you.

Claire Chidley

What is Energy Intelligence?

Chapter overview

This first chapter introduces the concept of Energy Intelligence (ENQ), locating it as a force which moves our intellect, creative, emotional and spiritual intelligence into action. Inspired by Einstein's Theory of Special Relativity, I consider its relevance to ENQ and its beneficial impact on the workplace. I highlight energy, motivation and commitment as crucial considerations for improving performance of both individuals and the whole team. I use two vignettes to illustrate the application of the ENQ formula, functioning well in "The Heart of the Matter" and functioning poorly in "The Red Bow Tie". I consider implications of ENQ for organisational leaders, managers, teams and individuals.

A New Aptitude: Energy Intelligence (ENQ)

Some years ago, I bought a book to read on a long train journey on route to a local authority where I was delivering a leadership development programme. The book was about the history of quantum physics. Perhaps to some, this wouldn't sound like a great read? But, I found it fascinating to learn about the nature of reality and how physics has shaped the world we live in today. Science has developed enormously over the last hundred years. Through mechanical and quantum physics, the behavioural sciences, molecular biology and neuroscience we have made giant leaps in our thinking about who we are, how we operate and the realities that we operate within. I was aware that some of the theories behind these great discoveries are being absorbed into management science, to greater or lesser effect, with the result of changing the way we understand people in work and how organisations develop. As I read the book, I considered whether the translation of scientific theories and terms into management practice could suggest alternative ways of improving people's performance and motivation? After all, as Nikolai Lobachevski, a Russian mathematician, born in 1792, wrote – "There is no branch of mathematics, however abstract, which may not someday be applied to phenomena of the real world." [1]

I decided they could and I set about looking at scientific terms, theorems and theories related to energy to inform this book's theory.

One of the most famous physics equations in the world is from Einstein's mass-energy equivalence formula arising from his Theory of Special Relativity which states $E=mc^2$ where E is energy, m is mass, and c is the speed of light in a vacuum.

According to Einstein, that the universal proportionality factor between equivalent amounts of energy and mass is equal to the speed of light squared. As the speed of light is 186,000 miles per second, that's pretty hard for anyone to grasp! Despite this, most people can remember the formula $E=mc^2$ although very few understand what it means. What is so great about Einstein's theory is that he was able to encapsulate something so incredibly sophisticated and complex into a simple set of letters which has stood the test of time with so many different scientific applications.

As the months passed, I began to think more about energy and mass and their broader application within the world. I considered the many uses and applications of the words *energy* and *mass*. Phrases like 'he drains my energy', 'I've got a mass of things to do', 'high energy' music, 'the mass of the people', came to mind. I also thought about the speeds at which we do different tasks and about how long it seems to take to do something we don't enjoy yet how quickly we tackle things when they motivate us.

It seemed to me that people are generally 'energy intelligent' in the sense they have an awareness of when they or the people around them have or don't have energy. They also understand how time seems to drag or speed up depending on the situation they are in.

Could there be a different type of 'intelligence' that we haven't understood related to an awareness of energy? Could this be additional to the many examples of 'intelligences' used today? I realised I'd stumbled on a new type of 'intelligence' related to energy which I named Energy Intelligence (ENQ in its abbreviated form).

I began to formulate my ideas. I developed distinctive characteristics related to leaders, managers and individuals. I also worked out ways to increase and decrease energy in the workplace depending on the prevailing conditions and how Energy Intelligence could be measured in individuals and applied to improve organisational performance.

Multiple Intelligences

Before I go into more detail about ENQ, let's take a brief look at the four key types of Intelligence known as *IQ, EQ, CQ,* and *SQ* that set Energy Intelligence in context.

The term 'IQ', (Intelligence Quotient) is a score devised from tests in the early twentieth century to measure people's mental intelligence. All the results from 'IQ' tests are added up and a mid-point is defined. People are then characterised as deviating above or below that mid-point with a high, low or average IQ. IQ scores can be used to predict educational achievement, job performance and income.

In the mid 1980's, the term Emotional Intelligence (EQ) was first used and this looked at the ability to identify, assess, and control the emotions of oneself, of others, and of groups. A range of personality profiles were developed to assess the level of emotional intelligence in individuals and teams.

At a similar time, Creative Intelligence (CQ) was developed to help people problem-solve, and to innovate. It helps people understand that we all have creative intelligence and can generate ideas and make connections between things.

Finally, the term Spiritual Intelligence (SQ) appeared at the end of the twentieth century. It is seen as the source that guides people's inner thinking and emotions and how they relate to the outside world to connect more deeply to make a contribution 'for' the world.

We are all made up of IQ, EQ, and SQ to varying degrees. Thoughts, feelings and beliefs exist within us (sometimes expressed on the outside of us) but they only become active **when energy is committed to them.**

The force that moves our thinking (IQ), behaviours (EQ) and beliefs (SQ) into action is called *Energy Intelligence (ENQ).*

14

I've described the contribution each of the intelligences IQ, EQ, CQ and SQ make in improving our conscious awareness and given a brief description of their unique characteristics. Now we know that Energy Intelligence exists, what are the constituent parts that make up ENQ and once known, how can they be applied in the workplace?

The Energy Intelligence (ENQ) Theory

Returning to that rail journey 'with Einstein', let me explain how my thinking has both deepened and crystallised since then, into the theory of Energy Intelligence, developed to improve workplace performance and productivity.

In my own work role as Director of a leadership development company where I train managers and teams, coach leaders and speak at or facilitate conferences, I've become aware that leaders, managers and individuals can be energetic (or not), that the flow of energy is strong and smooth (or not) and that there are marked differences in the pace and timing of work programmes.

Inspired by Einstein's Theory, I came to appreciate that the letters E, M and C may be used in an entirely separate way. The letters and words mean different things to me and can be used to create a theory for Energy Intelligence.

Let me explain more: The 'E' in Einstein's equation represents the 'energy of a body in movement'. To me, this could become the energetic state of people at work and how the workplace responds to change.

The 'M' of Einstein's equation means 'system' or 'mass'. In my interpretation, the M could represent the 'motivation' of the mass of people working within the system (or workplace). The best is brought out in people and their potential is realised depending on levels of individual and collective motivation.

'C' rather than representing the speed of light in a vacuum, in my equation, I understand it to represent people's commitment to their work and the way in which they discharge this commitment e.g. with a duty of care.

In my Energy Intelligence ENQ theory: **E=MCC**

'E' represents **Energy**, the power an individual and/or a group of people put into work and the force which results from this. In theory, the more energy that is put in, the greater the force created. Sometimes, a large amount of energy is put into work without much impact and energy is wasted. Conversely, small amounts of energy can be expended to great effect. In Energy Intelligence, a different way of thinking is needed to conserve energy and use it to its maximum effect. Workplaces with high ENQ can direct small amounts of energy purposefully to create a far greater thing or they could direct energy into something knowing it would produce a corresponding force. They also know to save energy or not expend any on certain things if they no longer serve a useful purpose.

These different forms of energy can be created and used to achieve a goal that efficiently uses the energy available in the workplace. These are considered later in this book in Chapters two and three.

'M' stands for **Motivation**, a stimulus that drives an individual towards a specific goal and it sustains the way the person behaves on that journey. In the case of Energy Intelligence, the motivation is driven from an inner desire to achieve an external goal and this desire is created from a stimulus of wanting to fulfil personal values and beliefs. It is important that the energy (in the form of skills, capabilities and resources) should be focused on activity aligned to the workplace vision, mission and values.

Motivation of this type is not driven by external reward or recognition, but if those things happen, it's a nice 'add on', not the means to the end.

'CC' corresponds to **Commitment** from *both* employers and employees (hence the double C!). Employers pledge a series of assurances to provide employees with an energetic and supportive working environment and employees dedicate themselves to deliver their work according to the workplace vision and mission and pledge to behave in line with workplace values. As the obligations and assurances are placed equally on the employer and employee, this creates a dual commitment to the workplace of employers to employees and vice versa.

Thus: *Energy = motivation multiplied by the commitment* of both employers and employees (E=MCC).

When the Energy Intelligence formula is applied in the workplace, it leads to improved performance and results and a further rise in energy, motivation and commitment leading to further sustained improvements in performance and results. In this way, the workplace becomes energy intelligent. It acquires the core capability of Energy Intelligence. It knows how to grow and use individual and collective energy to do something that everyone believes is important, that benefits the workplace, its customers and down the line, society at large. This is Energy Intelligence at work!

Fig 1. Emotional Intelligence in Action

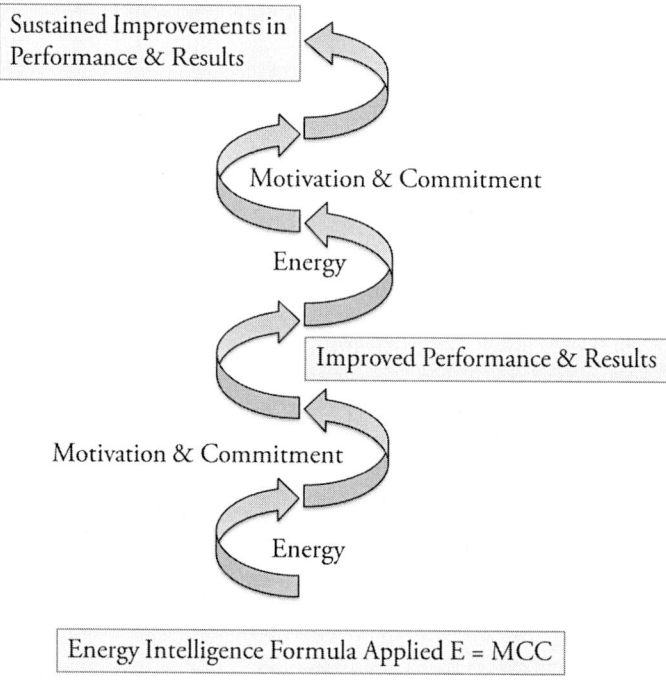

Imagine you are an athlete about to run in the Olympic 100 metres final. You've trained and worked hard for many years for this occasion, winning and losing races to be right here, right now. Your *vision* is to champion young people to follow in your footsteps. Your *mission* is to be the Olympic champion and your *goal*, to win this race. You know the journey is along the lane you have been given on the race track and you can see the destination, the finishing tape. You have even imagined what it would be like to have the gold medal placed over your head and to proudly stand to hear your national anthem. You are totally motivated and committed to the task ahead and you care completely about the outcome. You feel a surge of energy as the starter pistol fires and you run the race of your life.

Could the sprinter's performance and that of other athletes be improved using Energy Intelligence? If there was a way of improving the athlete's motivation and the commitment he puts into his work, would this create more energy and would this energy lead to further motivation, commitment improved performance and so on? Would this continue beyond the boundaries of what's possible to a new frontier (in his case a new world record speed over one hundred metres)? Of course it can!

Let me illustrate ENQ when it's working in a business context. Here are two stories. The first, 'The Heart of the Matter', shows applied Energy Intelligence. The second, 'The Red Bow Tie', reveals what happens when Energy Intelligence isn't used. The impact on leaders, managers, teams and individuals is shown in both instances.

The Heart of the Matter

The man slumped in the office chair slowly raised his eyes to the woman behind the desk

"Yes", was the only word she said.

"Thank you!" the other said, with feeling, and immediately left the room.

The woman at the reception desk saw him coming, and was ready, whatever the answer. She could see from his eyes that she could now make the call, forgot what she'd been doing and lifted the phone to set in motion a complicated string of events. No-one else knew how difficult it had been to pull together the various elements and to fine-tune the details, but she passionately wanted to get it right.

"Tell them I'm on my way" he called to her as he passed. As he joined his team and they began their work, time seemed to slow to a stop, but paradoxically, they were racing against it. They'd faced this challenge so many times before, but it never failed to inject a dose of adrenalin into his system. He felt it was a privilege to be here, an honour, and he mentally shared that sense of being special with the others in the team. Just for a moment, he thought about their counterpart team, preparing themselves several miles away, and wondered if they were feeling like this too.

One hour later he emerged. The drivers were waiting with the escort vehicles. Despite his tiredness the man couldn't help but see their eyes shining with excitement, as the package he carried was carefully stowed and the two vehicles pulled away into the night.

The drivers knew their mission. The responsibility was awesome, but never in their lives had they wanted it so much. Just to be able to make a difference, to contribute to such an achievement, made them focus on their journey with an intensity and dedication they rarely experienced in their daily routine. As they arrived at their destination, the anxious faces at the door relaxed and smiled. They delivered the package and sat down to wait.

Another team, another room, another challenge. The same frisson of fear mixed with excitement. As before, the hours race by and yet pass slowly, saturated with the intense concentration of the surgical team. They wait for the new heart to take its first beat.

The cheer was loud enough for the man slumped in the chair in the waiting room to hear. "YES!" was the only word he said, leaping up and punching the air (2).

What's happening here? Why are this team and the individuals within it so active, full of life and energised?

Here are some of the key reasons, expanded later in the book:

The Leader: A key decision is made that commits everyone to a course of action. An energetic response is thus created. The staff spring into action. Once the choice has been made, she doesn't alter it. She knows they are 'doing the right thing', that they are fulfilling their mission and purpose within a defined time-scale. Her role is to make the decision and then trust her manager to support the team to do its work. Her role is complete for now. She will not hamper or constrain them in any way. She gets involved again at the end to celebrate the team's success and should things have gone wrong, to step in and take ultimate responsibility for whatever failed. She will also ensure lessons will be learned of what worked well and less well.

Her use of Energy Intelligence involves making the key decision and being responsible for it. She commits the organisation from a state of *Rest energy* to *Total energy*. Then, she contains her own energetic response through the process, only releasing at the end. Until then, she plays the role of *Observer*. She waits for the result and is available if needed. This can be a lonely place because the connection to the action is detached, yet she is joined to the result. Despite the temptation to get involved and to find out what's going on, she remains stationery. When success is reported, she lets her energy out in an expression of joy.

What she is also aware of is that the team has consistently delivered successful outcomes like this and is showing signs of *Radiant energy*. In giving the gift of life to so many, the impact of this on families, workplaces and societies has been immense.

The Manager: He is the messenger who delivers his leader's decision. His role is to *manage energy flow* and he plays an active part in this. He 'rolls up his sleeves' and does his bit. He knows the complexity of the task needs a range of skills needed because he's been personally involved in their recruitment and ongoing development. In this scenario, each role played is critical and interconnected to the next, making everyone equally valuable. In the midst of the task, there is no hierarchy here. People don't defer to levels of seniority. The focus is on getting this job done and the team is doing it so well right now, he doesn't need to manage them. He will be there to encourage, support and make his contribution.

The Team: They are motivated to do well because they have an end goal and a defined time to achieve it. There is an awareness of an order of things, that one action follows from the previous one and this is completed almost unconsciously with a fluidity of motion that is finely synchronised. Their energy is positive and focused on the task, flowing towards the end result. Each team role is valued for without their input, no matter how small, the whole thing would fail. The sum of the individual parts of the team creates a greater whole and that greater whole is fulfilling its potential to achieve great things.

The Individual: The work they do is personally important. It resonates with their beliefs and values. They are committed to playing their part, no matter how small for they are doing something grander that makes the usual trials and tribulations in work unimportant. They are personally energised and that energy connects to the other team members. They are working both within their competency and are prepared to go beyond their capabilities should the need arise. Everyone shifts their time-frame away from past or future concerns to focus on the present, so nobody bickers; there are no petty jealousies on display or suggestions of a different or better way. The focus on the task and the concentration upon it is intense. This event is outside of the daily routine. It is not an everyday occurrence, but it happens on a regular basis.

Now, let's look at a different scenario of how things can go badly wrong when Energy Intelligence is not used.

The Red Bow Tie

The festival team are called to a meeting with the Leisure Director. The room is buzzing with nervous conversation and the Festival Manager senses her staff are apprehensive. If she'd been looking for evidence, it was all around her. She sits alone on the front row of chairs. Everyone prefers to sit at the back of the room as if by doing so they can avoid eye contact and any engagement with 'the Boss'.

The team has done well in her opinion. They've put together an exciting programme of cultural activities for the town's residents and visitors and are ready to start promoting it. The worrying thing was she has no idea why he's calling the meeting. As usual, the Director is being his usual 'opaque' self. Is he coming to praise his staff or tell them off she wonders?

Fifteen minutes after the meeting had been due to start, the Leisure Director sweeps into the room. So, it isn't a myth about his bow tie. Rumour has spread throughout the council that since the local elections have put a new political party in power, he's started wearing a red bow tie as if to broadcast his allegiance tied around his throat.

She feels sad that he must feel his position is so vulnerable that he's taken action that is making himself a laughing stock with staff. Her sadness soon shifts to anger when she remembers he's taken her paper on a new government policy and used it to speak at a national conference, passing it off as his own work. He's never given her any credit or acknowledgement.

Without any preamble or words of welcome, he begins speaking in a monotone. The energy in the room drops and her shoulders slump. She senses people fidgeting behind her.

"Good morning everyone. I've got some news for you. I'm setting you a new challenge." He says. "As of today, I'm reallocating the festival budget and putting it to good use on some new programmes in our leisure centres, so if you

want the festival to take place, you'll have to bring in enough sponsorship and ticket income to cover its costs."

She expects to hear a collective groan from her staff, not just because of the timing of his announcement but because the Director is showing yet again, favouritism towards other services in his portfolio and the low regard he holds towards them.

There is a deathly silence and the energy becomes palpable. It feels like a malevolent force is in the room and tenses as if waiting for the moment before prey lands on its quarry, but she no longer knows who is the hunter or the hunted.

She feels people's shock and anger and hoped nobody says what they are thinking because he'd never let them forget if they did.

Sensing the atmosphere in the room has changed, the Director seems nervous. He licks his lips and straightens his bow tie.

"That's good then. Everyone knows what to do. I'll leave it to you then". He nods briefly in the Festival Manager's direction and leaves the room.

The Manager thinks; 'He hasn't even bothered to explain why he's changed his mind or take questions, (not that he knows most of the staff by name or what they do).'

In the brief moment of silence that follows, the Festival Manager sits very still trying to conserve her energy. She wonders what on earth she will do next.

Then, the room erupts.

The Leader: He disrespects everyone by arriving late without apology or explanation. He has changed his mind and reversed a previous decision without giving any details as to why. This is quite usual for him. His leadership style is autocratic and that's that. His word is final. He has not briefed his manager before the meeting and as a result, has left her in a difficult position with her staff. She has no more knowledge than them and that makes her feel vulnerable and unsure. He makes no attempt to set a new direction, to motivate or engage with his staff or encourage ideas on how to take things forward. It seems the problem is theirs alone and he has wiped his hands of it. Worse still, his attitude plays into what people already believe about him (whether this is true or not); that he doesn't value what they do, that he favours other services and he is unsupportive of their efforts. His bow-tie reveals his career prospects are paramount and ironically, he has no idea they could be linked to the success of his colleagues.

He has some awareness of his high-handed manner and how oppressive this is. But he neither knows nor cares about how to alter it. Part of him enjoys the energy he creates of fear and uncertainty. People are just people and they can be replaced or worked around if they put up a fuss.

The Manager: She feels undermined by her leader. Her skills are not recognised by him, nor are the efforts of her team. He doesn't trust her views, her judgment or her experience. She's left with an impossible task. His timing is dreadful. If she'd been given a bit more notice, her team could have developed some solutions. She already doesn't trust or respect him and this is the final straw. In this environment, poor leadership isn't held to account and she's not going to put her head over the parapet to have it shot off. She feels drained by his attitude and manner and she can't see a way out. She's now left to deal with her team's anger and sadness and the resulting mayhem that will arise. In fact, she already is tired from working without his support and the gloomy feeling he's left her with makes her feel like going off on sick-leave.

The Team: As the situation unfolds, they are initially in shock. It is as if they are invisible and have no say in the matter. Then, they become angry with their manager for not telling them what the meeting was about and upset the Leader didn't explain things properly or answer the many questions they now have. If they'd been treated with respect and made to feel valued, they may have put energy into solving the problem. But they feel so de-motivated and flat, they can't be bothered. The whole thing is going to be a disaster, so far away from the exciting project they had committed to that would have made such a difference to their local community. As usual, 'management' were making a pig's ear of everything and they'd be on the receiving end of it all. How could they protect themselves from the 'you know what' that would hit the fan. Their focus was now on passing the buck and ducking to keep their heads down. They bear no responsibility for the outcome now. They don't care what happens.

The Individual: There is no sense that individual personalities or roles exist. You are a 'little person' with no power or way to express your view. The only person in the room who has a view is the Leader and his attitude and actions act like a *black hole* sucking all the energy out of the room and leaving people feeling drained, angry, confused and afraid.

The Heart of the Matter and *The Red Bow Tie* illustrate the extremes of Energy Intelligence at work. Most people have experienced to a greater or lesser degree, how energy in the workplace can impact on people's attitudes, outlook and behaviour and this can have a great impact on workplace motivation, performance, satisfaction, and success.

So now you know the basic theory and have read the stories about how ENQ operates, let's get 'under its skin' in the next three chapters to understand E=MCC better. Then you can learn how to apply it in work as a leader, manager or individual!

....

Now that you have read Chapter one, below are a few Energy Questions and points to consider:

1. Are you able to recognise the kind of energy that exists within: a) your organisation and b) the team with whom you work most closely?
    Is the energy that you describe constant, or does it vary? Try to describe the key features that come to mind.
    Are you aware of people, places and/or things that change the energy?

2. Having read "The Heart of the Matter" and the "The Red Bow Tie", do you recognise either or both of these scenarios in your workplace?
    Are you able to identify similarities with the leader, manager and team? If so, is this a new or established situation?
    How do you feel about this?
    How do you respond in this situation?

Make a few notes on ideas and thoughts that arise.

Chapter summary

Having introduced the concept of Energy Intelligence and its theory E=MCC, we have now considered the application of its formula into the workplace. One vignette "The Heart of the Matter" illustrates the wide-ranging benefits of its successful application, while a second, "The Red Bow Tie", presents the risks to an organisation when it is missing. In these two stories we have seen how energy, motivation and commitment are critical if the leader, managers, teams and individuals are to achieve high quality performance and results.

In the next chapter we will consider the importance of high "energy" within the application of ENQ to the workplace.

The Energy Spectrum

Chapter overview

This chapter introduces 'energy' as a dynamic concept within any workplace. It is recognised that pockets of high and low energy have considerable impact on activity levels and the health of an organisation and this is fundamental to understanding Energy Intelligence.

The characteristics of healthy, average and unhealthy energy states are described so that you may identify the presence or absence of these zones within the energetic spectrum of your own workplace. Movement along the spectrum is inevitable and 'The Stress Energy Tensor' offers a means by which leaders may identify whether energy levels (with associated motivation and productivity) are rising.

The Energy Zones

What is energy in the 'E' of my Energy Intelligence theory? What form does this energy take?

When you are in work, look around you and get a sense of the energy of your workplace. If it helps, walk around the building and note whether some areas are high or low energy and consider why that may be. Don't be fooled by whether the environment is noisy or quiet, sometimes, when individuals or teams are concentrating and not talking much, they could be expending a lot of energy in what they are focusing upon.

If your workplace feels low energy, it will be inactive, lethargic and sluggish. Worst case scenario, it seems like it is inert! Correspondingly, a high energy workplace will be lively, vigorous and dynamic.

Most places of work will have a mixture of low and high energy. There may be pockets of high or low energy and areas where energy is average or regular. If you reflect on this, you'll probably know who and where these are in your workplace!

Energy Blockages

A local authority Chief Executive once told me that one of his greatest leadership challenges in improving organisational performance was the application of a 'one size fits all' approach. To make things fair and give everyone equal opportunity to be trained, all managers attended the same training or performance management processes whether they needed it or not (and he noted the ones who needed it most made excuses to avoid attending.) Interventions were therefore not targeted to where they were needed most and a lot of time, effort and resources were wasted.

Due to ill health, he developed an interest in complementary medicine including the ancient arts of Reiki and acupuncture and he realised through them, something that had a profound impact on how he viewed work. He told me that he now saw that each of the councils he'd worked for were like a human being, each one with different personalities, behaviours, strengths and weaknesses and he now viewed each one *from an energetic perspective.* Using the human body as a metaphor, he explained that he could now see that one of the councils he'd worked in had energy blocked in the right arm and another in the left leg. He could now see a specific department or team was low energy and it was having an impact on the energy levels elsewhere in the body of the organisation. He suggested the solution; a course of treatment targeted at the part of the council where energy was blocked or low e.g. a staff, process, or system intervention that would have the same effect as using acupuncture to get the energy flow going and limb working to full use. His targeted approach would, in his view, have been more cost-effective than applying the same organisational development interventions throughout 'the whole body' of that council.

Figure 2 below represents the metaphor of his human body. (The white light on the body shows energy blockages and the darker areas energy flow and activity.)

Reflect on the corresponding parts of your workplace that are energy blocked or in flow.

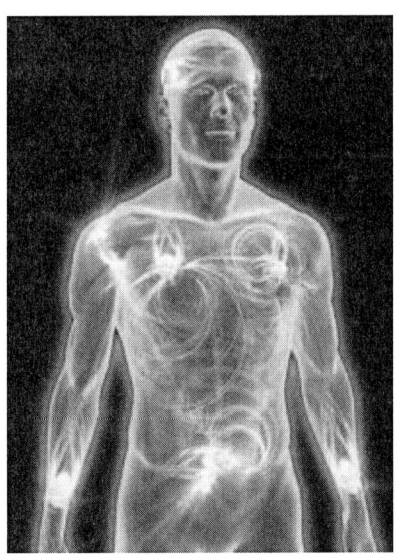

Fig 2. Blockages in the body

High Energy Zones at Work

Some workplaces operate with healthy energy. You experience a real 'buzz' about the place. People are sharing ideas, there's laughter and a focus on what's important. There's a sense of generosity, expansiveness and joy. According to psychologist Mihaly Csíkszentmihályi, when people are immersed in a feeling of energised focus and feeling fully involved and enjoying what they do, it is called 'flow'. They make tremendous progress, are hugely successful and high-performing in their field. They are trail-blazers, 'first movers' and set the pace for the rest of the pack. If this workplace in *flow* were a car, it would be a top of the range, highly maintained sports car!

In an interview with *Wired* magazine, Csíkszentmihályi described flow as "…being completely involved in an activity for its own sake. The ego falls away. Time flies. Every action, movement, and thought follows inevitably from the previous one, like playing jazz. Your whole being is involved, and you're using your skills to the utmost." (3)

Just like 'The Heart of the Matter', everyone seems to be 'in charge', in complete control of their work. There's a sense that the unfolding day and the days to come are going to be great and that all will be well. There's a lightness of being in the staff.

In rare cases of high energy, workplaces reach a state Csíkszentmihályi calls *Hyperfocus,* where the organisation lights up because it is so focused on something specific and significant. Walter Isaacson, Biographer of Steve Jobs the Co-Founder of Apple commented on his legendary ability of Hyperfocus: "When Jobs returned to Apple in 1997, it was producing a random array of computers and peripherals, including a dozen different versions of the Macintosh. After a few weeks of product review sessions, he'd finally had enough. "Stop!" he shouted. "This is crazy." He grabbed a Magic Marker, padded in his bare feet to a whiteboard, and drew a two-by-two grid. "Here's what we need," he declared. Atop the two columns, he wrote "Consumer" and "Pro." He labelled the two rows "Desktop" and "Portable." Their job, he told his team members, was to focus on four great products, one for each quadrant. All other products should be cancelled. There was a stunned silence. But by getting Apple to focus on making just four computers, he saved the company. "Deciding what not to do is as important as deciding what to do," he told me. "That's true for companies, and it's true for products."(4)

When high energy and Hyperfocus come together, they create 'Radiant Energy' which is described in more detail on page 66.

Average Energy Zones at Work

Most workplaces lie somewhere in the middle of the energetic spectrum. They make steady progress; the atmosphere is congenial and upbeat. Energy levels are generally healthy. Sometimes, there are 'ups' and 'downs' over the course of the year and when these occurrences happen, energy is put into getting things 'back on track.' Nobody quite knows what this means because the workplace doesn't have a strong vision or mission, so it's something about 're-finding our comfort-zone'. There is ambition to do a bit better, to stretch out a bit, but if that doesn't happen, it's not the end of the world. There's a false sense of security here. For as the average-energy workplace will never be motivated to reach the dizzying heights of the high-energy workplace and more worryingly, it could easily drop into the unhealthy energy state.

On the margins of the average energy workplace, there are a rump of the work-shy, the disgruntled, the weary and the stressed. These people are anxious about their position and their future. They feel adrift in a non-strategic sea and don't feel they are honouring their values. Their healthy energy lies untapped and their unhealthy energy begins to leech into the wider workplace, affecting the work of others. Average and healthy energy people start to wonder why they are making the effort when others aren't. If this workplace were a car, this would be a comfortable, well-used people carrier with worn tyres and faulty seatbelts just about to go for an MOT!

Low Energy Zones at Work

This is a place nobody wants to be in for long! Morale has dropped. People have given up trying. They don't care anymore. Relationships are fractured. Leadership is lacking. There's confusion and chaos about priorities as there are too many. There's high absenteeism and sickness, putting more pressure on those who remain in work. People are leaving the sinking ship. Those who remain become lonely and cut-off. Isolated energy is produced. People don't share their ideas or work together as 'knowledge is power' and in this 'look after number one' atmosphere, becomes toxic. Beyond this point, it's a downward spiral. The workplace is *Radioactive*.

If this were a car, this workplace would be an old banger that is being towed to the scrap yard before it causes an accident!

Figure 3 opposite shows the spectrum of characteristics seen in high, average and low workplace zones and the words that describe their energetic state. This is called *The Energy Spectrum*.

Fig 3. The Energy Spectrum

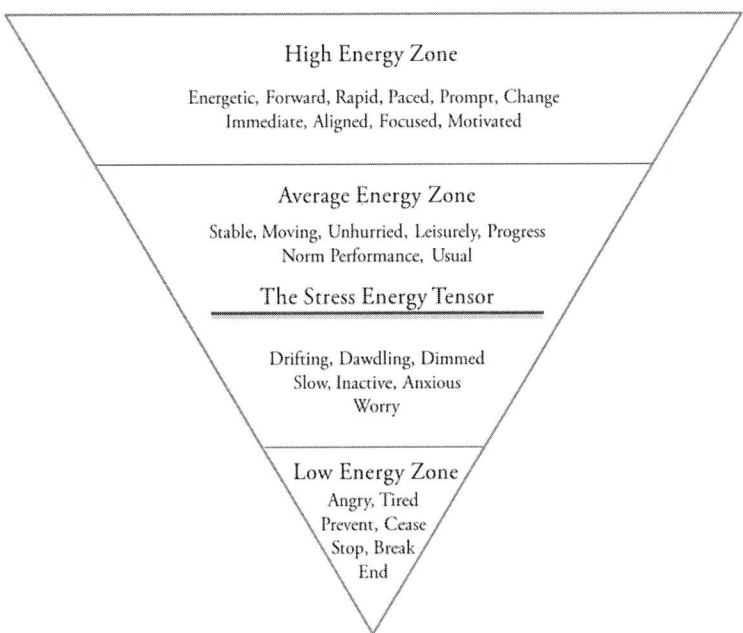

If you aren't sure where you are on the spectrum, try this test out with your colleagues. Ask them to describe in one word how they are when they are feeling 'healthy', 'average' and 'unhealthy'. Quite often, you will hear phrases like 'buzzing', 'happy', 'focused for healthy, 'OK', 'chugging along', contented for average and 'tired', 'bored', 'disengaged' for unhealthy. When you have their three words, ask them on a normal week, which word best describes how they are and whether they believe this describes their workplace. You should be able to place their words into the spectrum.

The Stress Energy Tensor

Figure 4 below shows the point at which positive energy becomes negative. It is when average energy levels drop towards the low energy zone. I call this place *The Stress Energy Tensor*. In physics, this is a quality that describes the density and flux of energy and momentum in space-time. It is an attribute of matter, radiation and non-gravitational force-fields.

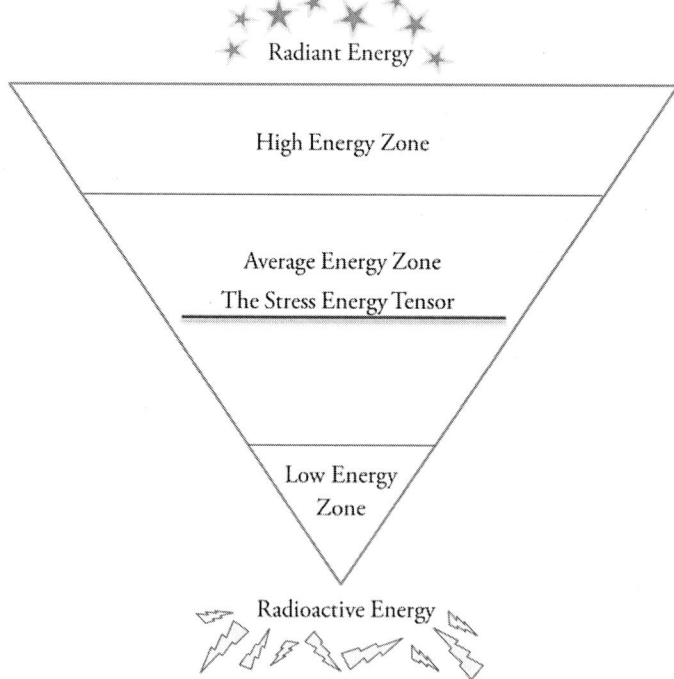

Fig 4. The Stress Energy Tensor

In the workplace, as The Stress Energy Tensor point is reached, energy loses its quality of lightness of being, becoming denser and more unstable. This happens due to two primary reasons:

1. The workplace energy 'over-heats' because it can't sustain a level of high energetic response. It hasn't employed strategies to come off the pace and rest. As a result, it burns out and falls rapidly to the bottom of the spectrum where there's a lot of 'radiation' and toxicity. Here, it's hard for a workplace to recover or survive.

2. A lack of clarity (similar to the excerpt on page 32 where Apple was heading prior to Steve Job's intervention) around strategic priorities and 'drift' away from workplace vision and mission causes 'force-fields' to emerge within individuals and teams. People are doing too many conflicting things and none of them particularly well. Leaders aren't leading and because of this, workplace aims are unclear and staff place their own interpretation on what they think is important. Instead of people operating freely within one coherent strategic force-field, many smaller fields are created that chafe against each other. Performance drops and energy levels begin their downward spiral.

In a rare interview on his thoughts about leadership, Peter Drucker notes, "Effective leaders check their performance. They write down, "What do I hope to achieve if I take on this assignment?" They put away their goals for six months and then come back and check their performance against goals. This way, they find out what they do well and what they do poorly. They also find out whether they picked the truly important things to do. I've seen a great many people who are exceedingly good at execution, but exceedingly poor at picking the important things. They are magnificent at getting the unimportant things done. They have an impressive record of achievement on trivial matters" [5].

As the workplace moves down the Energy Spectrum, lower energy states develop and you will note from figure three what kinds of behaviour to look out for. In most cases, the descent is gradual, until at a certain point (and this will vary workplace to workplace), the negative energy grows and eventually becomes greater than the size of the organisation. At this point, people in the external environment will hear what an awful workplace it is or the products and services are poor. This negative energy is the direct opposite to that explained in the section on *Radiant Energy* (see the next chapter). Instead of the workplace creating positive energy that influences and changes the external environment, the workplace pumps out damaging 'Radioactive' energy that can be destructive to the well-being of staff, customers, the operating environment and company reputation. Atrophy then occurs. The workplace weakens and degenerates and in extreme circumstances, ceases to exist.

Workplaces who want to stay healthy and to move up Energy Zones use their knowledge of positive energies through their understanding of motivation and commitment. This is *applied Energy Intelligence.*

．．．．．．．．．．．．．．．．．．．．．．

Having read Chapter two, here are a few Energy Questions to consider:

1. Can you recognise healthy, average and unhealthy energy states within your organisation as a whole, or within your direct team?
2. If so, what do these look like? Try to describe their features.
3. How is your morale and that of your colleagues?
4. How is productivity?

5.   Might any of these states be noticeable by 'others' e.g. partners, customers, clients etc?

Chapter summary

A recognition that energy states vary within an organisation, its teams and individuals is a vital component in understanding its performance. In this chapter we have identified the characteristics of healthy, average and unhealthy zones within The Energy Spectrum and the potential risks that emerge from the latter state.

In the next chapter we will explore the application of a range of positive energies within the workplace, helping to lift it higher within the Energy Zones.

CHAPTER 3

The Five Energies

Chapter overview

In this chapter the importance of a range of five 'Positive energies' that can be harnessed within an organisation are considered. These vary in type: Potential energy exists within core capabilities, waiting to be released yet also reminds us of the necessity of restorative Rest energy; Kinetic (moving) energy that can be focused and goal-directed; Elastic energy that can yield, stretch and accommodate change can focus and concentrate energy and Radiant energy that will transfer and transform activity into the wider environment.

These positive energies are discussed in relation to the workplace, continuing to identify methods that will help to move an organisation up through The Energy Spectrum.

Think of the light emitted by a 100 watt light bulb. Each watt from a laser beam is 100,000 times more powerful. The power from directed energy has phenomenal potential. The art of Energy Intelligence when practiced over time is to know how, when, and in what quantity to apply this power to an activity. (Anyone who practices a martial art will learn that they can generate power and speed with little effort because they are working with the force of energy which they call *chi*).

Understanding the five 'Positive Energies', how and when to apply them increases exponentially, your power of focus within the workplace. They also lift your workplace up the Energy Zones.

In this chapter, there are five different kinds of energy to be aware of. Each one strengthens the 'E' in E=MCC and can be used to move your workplace forwards.

---

1 - Potential Energy

Potential energy is energy stored within an object positioned in a gravitational, electric or magnetic field. This is energy that is not in motion or being used, but has the *potential* to be used. In any workplace, the potential energy is found in the skills, knowledge and experience of staff, a culmination of the work they have already undertaken together with their broader life experiences. Potential energy is different in every workplace because of the unique skill-set and knowledge that staff bring to a place (often described as a core capability.) Only a fraction of this potential energy is used. Most of it is lying dormant, hidden from sight.

Why is this important? If more of this potential energy could be identified and harnessed, it would make a powerful impact on workplace performance as it holds in check the 'magnetic-field' of your workplace aspirations e.g. your vision, mission and their not yet delivered programmes.

Here are two examples of potential energy.

Example one:

At short notice, I was told that a group of Japanese business people wanted to visit our town with a view to opening up a factory. I wanted to greet them properly, even speak a little Japanese. So, I emailed my staff asking if they had experience of the Japanese customs and language. To my surprise, a number of staff came forward. (One could speak Japanese quite well as he'd taught English in Japan some years before.)

I learned how to greet my guests and a few phrases of Japanese and they were delighted with my efforts. If I hadn't needed something and then asked the question, I would never have known this knowledge existed in my workplace.

Example two:

After meeting with a Health and Safety Manager to appraise her of a piece of work I was doing in her workplace, we went for a coffee. I asked her: "It must be a real challenge being the person responsible for health and safety. How do you persuade the staff to take on board what they need to do when they are so busy?" She told me: "In a previous 'incarnation', I was a Head of Department in a large college, so I learned how to fight my corner over funding and I managed a lot of people. I've learned how to be assertive and persuasive!" When I asked her if her colleagues knew she had these skills and were they being used now in the workplace, she replied, "No. And it makes me sad I can't use this knowledge and experience more here."

I always start my training sessions with a usual: 'Tell me your name and what you do' question. Often, I ask people to tell me 'one interesting thing about you!' You'd be amazed at the things people come up with! One memorable response was a man who said he'd been a personal bodyguard to a very famous politician and an author. When I asked him; "So are you licensed to kill?" he said; "Not anymore!" His colleagues (who had worked with him for five years), had no idea about his previous career. The coffee break was certainly interesting! It shows how much potential energy there is in your workplace, and how it is 'at rest' and you probably don't even know it's there!

Here are some reasons why potential energy may be 'hidden' in your workplace:

- Managers don't know or ask about the broader skills, knowledge and experience of their staff.
- Managers tend to ask energetic, engaged staff to do work, not the lethargic and disengaged.
- Performance of the lethargic and disengaged staff isn't properly tackled. Nobody asks why people are like this and how they can support them to improve.
- The recruitment process doesn't cover anything wider than the skills and experience needed to do the job.
- Employee engagement is poor so people don't volunteer information.
- People avoid coming forward because it will add to their workload.
- Managers and staff don't negotiate what to give up, to take on something new.
- Everyone is suffering from work fatigue because the workplace vision is unclear and/or priorities keep changing.
- The pace of work is not being set. It feels manic and people are stressed.

If potential energy could be developed by utilising it for activity in the workplace, people would feel fully engaged and used and energy levels would rise.

Whilst this might be a bit ambitious for most workplaces, here are some simple, cost-effective ways you can develop some of the Potential Energy you aren't using or are aware of.

- When recruiting staff, ask them to provide broader information about their prior experience, even if it doesn't seem relevant to the job they are applying for.
- Ask people to contribute to a central Potential Energy file (logged centrally on open access). The file could contain details 'things you didn't know about me' e.g. hobbies and interests, languages spoken, wider work experience and volunteering. (At worst, you may have enough musicians for a workplace band or actors for a Christmas pantomime!)
- Create a workplace 'think-tank' made up of a cross-section of staff. Set them a challenge to meet for a day every three months to assess future in business critical programmes for potential weaknesses in resources to be engaged, staff involvement, product development and launch.
- Have a workplace 'critical friend' who is not an expert in the future programme or project to ask for it to be explained in 'lay-man's' terms, posing any questions that arise.
- Add into annual staff surveys questions on 'the energy of our place'. Ask where they feel energy levels are too high (or too low) or blocked, why and what could be done to sort them.
- Use the model of "lunch and learn" sessions, where staff have the opportunity to examine a team's work, a project or programme objectively e.g. a case study, learning what went well or could have been done better-accompanied by lunch!
- Road shows can also be helpful, but they should be used to discuss core issues and facilitated by the CEO to ensure maximum staff participation.

- Give staff time off to do activities to support their local community, to learn something new and make different connections.

Harnessing potential energy has two additional benefits. One of the benefits is once energy starts to move, *'Kinetic energy'* is created (see page 51). Another is that the capabilities people learned from other life experiences may be able to add some 'stretch' if there's a gap in resources needed to fulfil the task. As potential energy starts to be used, and combined with other energies explained further in this chapter, overall energy in the workplace becomes more powerful and directed.

---

2 - Rest Energy

Understanding Rest Energy is crucial to the measured releasing of Potential energy. If all the energy stored in the workplace is used all of the time, it will overheat, blow or burn out (think of leaving an iron on constantly!). Whilst we want to use the potential energy, it's also important to know when to 'power down' and rest.

Why does this matter? So many people run from one piece of work to the next or multi-task a number of complex projects. The focus of their energy is dissipated and diluted and this affects the success of the work and the performance of the individual and team. (Think back to the story 'The Heart of the Matter' once more. If you had to do that day in, day out, it wouldn't be long before you and everyone else felt exhausted!). If this pace were kept up indefinitely, the system/workplace would become a *negative mass*, measured in rising employee sickness levels, lower employee engagement, higher staff turnover and dropping down to the lower levels of The Energy Spectrum.

Yet people carry on regardless of their personal health or that of the workplace because it's addictive! The speed of work triggers a 'fight or flight' response to the stress and an adrenaline rush is the reward. When there's no let up because the pace of work doesn't slow down, the adrenalin rush can in itself become harmful. Cortisol (the stress hormone) is released into the bloodstream and is usually an effective way of calming and relaxing the body's response to stress, returning the body's functions to normal. Unless there's time to relax, the body's stress response is activated so often that the body doesn't always have a chance to return to its regular rhythm, resulting in a chronic state where low energy, motivation, performance and depression can result. In times of recession, people also feel they have to 'over-perform' as they are worried about keeping their jobs.

It's important that once a project or programme of activity is complete there is rest time. Everyone needs to take a break, to relax, recharge their batteries and reflect on the work concluded to understand the lessons learned. In many workplaces, the pace of work is so frantic and dysfunctional. Often, there's a cultural belief that if you are seen to be idling or doing nothing, you aren't being productive. Making yourself busy might keep your job, but it isn't going to increase your productivity or give you the space to be creative, learn from your work and try out new ideas.

So, we need Rest energy. Everyone should get away from their work for a little while, to a place where they can quietly think for a bit, even to gain inspiration. The whole idea is to break up work routines, to think about why you are doing things, rather than how or what and to consider 'could it be possible there's a better, quicker, more efficient way of doing this?'

A new idea generated in this space could save time, money, resources and energy further down the line.

There are plenty of examples of companies and organisations that have 'gone bust' or turned from being good/fair performers into rescue cases for government inspectorates. Behind the headlines of money poorly invested, technology changes that didn't work and workplaces not adapting to changing consumer demand are workplaces where Rest energy wasn't being applied. Neither was Potential energy fully explored and used.

Michael Roche, founder of the successful Andid International Diamond Corporation uses his prior experience as a Buddhist monk to work with Rest energy. "I'd like to describe...another trick that the great Tibetan wise men use to maintain their physical health, and a high degree of mental creativity, over the long term. It's not unusual to find Tibetan monks in their sixties and seventies who display an ever-increasing intellectual appetite and curiosity, who are physically able to maintain long hours and skip downstairs in a way that people in the West have lost by the time they are forty.

The trick is called *tsam*. Tsam in Tibetan means 'border' or 'dividing line', and the word is used to describe the art of getting away from your work every once in a while-going off somewhere else and, in a sense, drawing a circle around yourself where you can think quietly for a bit." (6)

The Simplyhealth Group based in Andover, Hampshire, has annual turnover in excess of £350m a year. It was featured in the Sunday Times 100 Best Companies to Work for 2007 (7). In addition to extensive learning and development programmes, the company gives staff time off to join in community projects and voluntary programmes. This has included supporting the Vision for Andover and clearing local rivers and streams.

Some workplaces focus on creating restful spaces to encourage down time and an environment to imagine and think creatively. In his fascinating article, 'Top 20 Most Awesome Company Offices,' Josh Dunlop talks about mobile phone provider Dtac. "Dtac recently decided to put an end to separate office spaces throughout the city of Bangkok, and brought all six buildings under one roof, which happens to be the largest ever office lease in Thailand's history, occupying around 650,000 square feet. The move and design reflects the company's desire to become the employer of choice, to "enhance cooperation and communication, strengthen common goals, increase creativity" and make it easier for the brand to react quickly to changing conditions.

Dtac's brand approach is "play and learn" and they wanted to reflect this to their employees and customers with their new, rather inspiring office, spanning 22 floors. Some of the highlights include a massive circular library amphitheatre, and an entire floor dedicated to fun, with indoor soccer, table tennis, running track, and concert and performance spaces. To feed creativity, there's the Conversation Pit, the Freeform Meeting, Picnic Table and Dining Room, all created to encourage informal, face-to-face meetings. And let's not forget what tops off the building – an open terrace overlooking Bangkok's skyline." (8)

Here are some ways you can create Rest energy.

- Develop a similar space called 'Rest energy Room' where all staff can go for up to 30 minutes a day to sit, be still and reflect. The time should be consistent (e.g. at 10am) and the commitment should never be broken whatever is going on in work or needs to be done. The room should be decorated in warm, but muted colours and have comfortable furniture to relax in. Apart from fresh water, it shouldn't provide magazines, drinks or music. This is a space to 'get away from it all'.

- Encourage exercise and relaxation in the workplace. (Two of the best things I ever did to relax in work was to take part in a weekly Tai Chi class and to have a monthly chair massage).
- Provide staff with an annual fitness and health check-up looking at blood-pressure, cholesterol and blood sugar levels. (From this a number of staff maybe identified to have ill-health ranging from mild to serious, so it's a useful 'early warning system').
- Taking light exercise. A walk around the workplace for 15 minutes in a sanctioned break will relax the body and mind as well as providing other health benefits.

For the Individual:

- In bed before you go to sleep, review the day just passed. Check for the 3 best things you said or did and the worst 3. Concentrate on the three good things as you go to sleep.
- Find a place in your home which is safe and relaxing. Spend 10 minutes each morning before you go to work sitting in this place and having a silent time. Take your mind to the coming day and mentally role-play your work, meetings and conversations. Imagine your interactions are full of positive energy.
- Keep a brief journal in written or virtual form of your thoughts and ideas.

Too Much Rest Energy!

Finally, there's an 'elephant in the room' that should be addressed. Many staff in your workplace are in their forties and fifties. They may have been working for twenty or thirty years. Some may not be ambitious and even if they are, they probably know they won't make it any higher up the 'greasy pole' and can see younger people with more energy and potential, running up fast on their heels.

Work has become boring and they are dulled by it. They are taking Rest energy literally! This is called Negative Rest Energy. These colleagues are coasting or cruising in neutral. They know what to do but they are applying the minimum amount of effort in doing it.

What can you do about them? They need a fresh challenge, something they can do in parallel to the 'day job' and that needs leaders and managers to put some thought into this. (Chapter 4: Motivation will help a lot in solving this issue).

3 - Kinetic Energy

In physics, a common energy form is the kinetic energy of a moving object. The more the object moves, the more kinetic energy it generates. Kinetic Energy is also known as 'energy in motion.'

Imagine you roll a small rock down a hill. You exert a bit of energy to start the rock moving. As it rolls down the hill, it gains its own momentum and moves faster and faster towards its destination. Yet, the energy used at the beginning is only a small fraction of the speed used by the rock on its descent and the energy this creates. This is Kinetic Energy. Another example: Think of a spaceship travelling into space. It uses up a terrific amount of energy to leave the earth's orbit. Due to gravitational pull, the kinetic energy build up to do this is so great, that once the ship enters into space, it generates momentum to travel at a rate which is more than the energy required. This 'slingshot' effect powers the ship with it using the minimum amount of fuel. (This in a more complex form is how space agencies believe we will be able to travel to Mars in the future!)

Focusing at the onset on how you will use your energy to best effect and then making an intervention to 'start the ball rolling' will produce kinetic energy momentum using less energy over the whole journey. If the destination is decided and mapped out and nobody alters course, journey's end will be reached with energy to spare.

Why does this matter? In workplace terms, deciding to take a course of action will cause movement, shifting 'the energy of the place'. In fact, any course of action will do this. Some actions may not be helpful, (especially if they aren't aligned to your vision and mission). You could in fact be doing a lot of work too little effect and instead of moving forwards, you could be moving backwards, sideways or even downwards! In Energy Intelligence, any movement has to have focus and intention so the energy you employ and the 'Kinetic energy' generated moves the work forward to the end goal.

Here's an example of how countries took a different approach to solving a major problem. Some expended a lot of energy and wasted a lot of effort. Others used very little energy, yet the end result was the same but the costs varied tremendously. The difference was in understanding what the real focus and intention should be. Without that focus, the advantages of Kinetic energy were not exploited by some nations.

In the mid 1990s, people got worried that when the millennium approached, computers wouldn't be able to recognise the year 2000 and would stop working. The problem became known as 'the Millennium Bug'. Companies in the UK spent an estimated £25 billion and a lot of energy into upgrading computer systems; more per head than any other country in the world. *"The clock duly struck midnight and ... nothing happened, no global crisis, no economic meltdown. The world continued to turn".* (9)

Yet, other countries like Brazil averted the crisis by changing the dates on their computers because they simply couldn't afford to pay for consultants to do the work!

So was the Millennium Bug just 'hype' to work people up enough to pay a lot of money out to computer experts or was it a serious issue and we were right to take precautions? *"It is probably impossible ever to know the real extent of the millennium bug simply because we cannot go back and run the whole thing again without taking any precautions. It may have been a huge success of global cooperation and understanding, or the biggest fraud in history."* (9)

Think of all the activities that are started by well-meaning people in your workplace that peter out because there isn't a clear purpose for them and people aren't personally committed. In my own experience, doing work I didn't believe in and couldn't see the point of always failed (if it ever got off the starting blocks)!

When I was in charge of an adult education service, government funding changed which meant that so called 'leisure' classes (courses that didn't give you a qualification at the end) were not going to be subsidised. This meant that the courses would only run if fee income covered their cost. I was unhappy about this because I believed 'leisure courses' were a route through into formal learning and I was concerned a lot of people wouldn't be able to afford the new rates. My staff felt the same, yet we had to implement the new ruling or be subject to various penalties. So you can imagine how much energy went into performing this task. We operated from the *Average Energy Zone* bordering on the *Low Energy Zone* at times and used a lot of *Rest energy* in the process! It took us much longer to perform the task than we would have done if we'd believed in what we were doing!

So, Kinetic energy power cannot be sustained unless it has a powerful focus of intention. (The intention is to decide to roll *that* rock down *that* specific hill)! The centre of attention is provided by the workplace mission and vision and the team working their way through the 'What Why' process described on the next page. These factors build in meaning and direction to energy creation, its flow and sustainability.

To get the system to move and move on the right track, you need to decide the destination, the direction you want to take to get there *and* control the speed you want to travel at.

It's surprising how many workplaces don't have a vision/direction of travel (or if they do, they don't pay heed to it.) Leaders need to set the workplace mission and vision and this should not be put out to wider consultation in the workplace. The workplace mission and vision is a fundamental remit of the CEO. If they consult with anyone, it should be their Board, elected representatives, probably shareholders and possibly, their leadership team.

I explain more about how to do this in the next chapter, *Mission & Vision* and Chapter 7 *Energy Intelligent Leaders*. That said; managers and teams can also play a role in creating 'mini-missions' and mini-visions' for their work and this can be done any time within the context of the overarching mission and vision for the workplace through my 'What Why' process.

Creating Kinetic Energy through the 'What Why' Process

Before anyone starts a new work-stream or project, they should use my *What Why* process. In asking and answering up to ten simple questions, the focus and intention of what's required is understood before a lot of energy is expelled. It will also mean that once the project is 'on the go', Kinetic energy is created and will continue to be released until the project is completed.

Here are the ten questions a team should ask before embarking on any new activity.

1. What's the purpose of this work?
2. Why are we doing it?
3. Why is it important?
4. What value will we add? (Depending on your workplace mission, value could mean increased income, improved usefulness, increasing respect, raising esteem.)
5. Why does this work 'fit' with our workplace mission and vision?

If you get a 'no' to any of the first five questions don't begin the work. If you are clear about all of them, then ask yourself five more 'what's'.

6. What will this work look like when it's completed?
7. What time-scales does it need to be completed by?
8. What needs to be done?
9. What people should we involve?

10. What have we not considered?

Most fundamental of all, is how little time is spent on Question 6. Many times I've sat as the project sponsor with a team who tell me they want to develop such and such project. When I ask them 'what will it look like' e.g. how will things flow better for the end-users, they haven't got a clue! Once, when I was asked to approve a half a million pound budget for an electronic documents records management system, nobody on the project team had thought through how the final product would work *in practice* and what people (staff and customers) could expect from it.

Big IT projects seem to be prone to this. We've all heard about the tremendous amount of money, energy and time spent on NHS, ambulance, air-traffic, benefits systems that fall short of expectations.

Arthur Murphy, a Director in PricewaterhouseCooper's programme and change management practice gives a great example of what I mean.

"When a company decides to invest in new technology it is easy to lose sight of the business case for implementation - with expensive consequences..... One common problem is that many IT projects fail to win the support of end-users before new software or hardware is rolled out. Experience in the IT market provides plenty of examples of this kind of problem.

Take the life insurance company that wanted to increase sales. It initiated a project to provide its salespeople with laptops. It provided bespoke software to gather and analyze information to select the right product and generate policy documents, all in the clients' homes. The salespeople liked the technology and the substantial time saved through this. How-

ever, management noticed no significant increase in sales and discovered that many salespeople worked to a specific earnings level, and once it was achieved, did not pursue extra sales. This is a classic example of a single-minded focus on the IT goal - introduce new laptops and tailored software - rather than the business benefits of a project - improving productivity.

Technology enables business improvement, it is not the end-goal. The system delivered by IT at the life insurer worked perfectly, but the project failed to increase sales volumes, which was the true goal."(10)

The 'What Why' process isn't hard, but it can be time-consuming if you have a lot of staff, but I believe it's one of the most important things that should be done and the process should be repeated by a manager with their staff every time a team begins a project. The same questions can be used at staff appraisal times to assess performance and to plan for the year ahead. Being focused on work that matters and having to justify that it does, will make a huge difference to the energy of your workplace.

It appears that 'nothing is being done' whilst 'What Why' is going on. Not so. In addition to stepping back and reflecting, you may save money and people energy and time overall. You are also allowing yourself a bit of Rest energy and possibly revealing some Potential energy you didn't know you had!

My 'What Why' process is critical in building up and focusing workplace energy because once it makes any resulting action 'energetically intelligent'. You know what is about to be done and why. Moving forward according to an agreed course of action accelerates the 'body' (workforce) and as the project begins, Kinetic energy is created. Kinetic energy builds incrementally at a steady pace through each stage of the project and will gain a momentum of its own. As this momentum is anticipated, energy can be re-deployed into other tasks in the project. For example, once we started getting other people offering to help us with the Central Library project (which I describe in detail on the next page - *Elastic Energy*), I was able to move staff away from certain tasks (interior design) and onto others (ordering books, and media items).

Sometimes, projects have to be speeded up, slowed down or put on hold. Kinetic energy in action means that if things needed to be speeded up (to meet a changed deadline or increased demand for example), as momentum is already building in its own right, it will take a small burst of energy to increase the speed of the project. This can quickly be found by seeking out further Potential energy in the workforce or employing 'stretch' as a tactic (see 4 Elastic Energy). Ultimately, the Kinetic energy may turn into Radiant energy (see 5 Radiant Energy on page 66) at the project's end.

If it's decided suddenly to slow down or stop the programme, energy may have to be removed more dramatically because it has developed a speed of its own. Often, a lot of work and energy has to take place to decelerate the project from its current speed to a state of rest. Sometimes, it's going to take as much energy to slow the activity down or work until it stops as it would to keep it going. The team may need to deploy other forms of energy e.g. Elastic energy.

This is why people feel tired or drained when priorities change. They have used a lot of energy to get the project in motion and still use a significant amount to slow it down or stop it. When leadership decisions chop and change, the workforce feels chopped and changed!

The effort put into the 'What Why' process will set the right course of action and accelerate movement in the direction of travel that's been determined. If it's decided a project is of priority importance and it has to be completed to a specific time (just like the story of the transplant teams in 'The Heart of the Matter'), teams decide the speed it should happen by and managers can set and keep a check on the pace. Once the project is up and running, it will take on a life of its own, kinetic energy is produced and the benefits of increased momentum will result in energy savings across the project.

4 - Elastic Energy

In a new job as Head of Culture for the council in Poole, my brief was to develop libraries, arts, museums and archives. I recall that when I first met the Central Library staff, whilst I believed them to be lovely people, I could tell they were worn down by the dreadful building they worked in. The library was huge. It had originally been built to house a bowling alley and that project had never come to anything. I doubt the building had ever been decorated since its completion. The walls where a ghastly pink; (I over-heard someone say 'baby-bottom pink' and that seemed very accurate!) The furniture looked tired and dated and the place didn't feel like a location for encouraging curiosity, learning and progression.

I don't recall my exact words, but I suddenly found myself announcing; 'By this time next year, we will have a refurbished library, a space you and people in Poole will be proud to use". No pressure there then!

The reaction I got was a weary '*Yeh yeh,*' because everyone didn't believe it would happen. I'd rashly made a commitment and on re-flection, I realised that I'd put my neck on the line and my reputation where the whole service would now rise or fall on my ability to deliver.

But how and where would I begin? Looking at my library management team, one colleague had more energetic 'get up and go' than the others and I noticed she had a great rapport with the staff. I asked her to help me lead the project and she agreed. She was bored and needed a 'parallel challenge to her day job'. I then targeted the elected representative, the Councillor who was responsible for my service. He was enthused by my energy and said he would get support at his committee to release repairs and maintenance funding for the project. It was a handy sum of money and in my naivety I assumed it might do the trick.

At times when I'm unsure, you already know I revert to support from my family. My mother made an insightful comment about the energy of the workplace she visited in the preface to this book. In this instance, I decided to 'keep it in the family' by asking my uncle Bill to come and look over the library. He is a retired architect and an incredibly talented man.

We walked all around the building and as we did, he asked me for my vision of the place, what I wanted it to look like, sound like and feel like when it was finished. Most importantly of all, he asked me about the energy of the new place and where the quiet and more lively spaces would be.

When we'd finished, he said; "Well, to get what you want, you'll need about 15 times more money than you have." I was crestfallen. It was impossible. Poole Council was a small authority, money was tight and what was needed was a huge sum. It wasn't going to happen.

He turned to me and held my arm. Looking directly into my eyes, he said: "When you have a great idea, the money will follow. Just trust you are doing the right thing."

Something happened inside me. I felt a surge of energy, excitement and will-power. Despite the prevailing environment and all the obstacles, I would persevere.

And I did. Over the coming months, I met as many people as I could, selling the vision of how the library could be. My staff became enthusiastic and we developed the vision in detail through my 'What Why' process. Other staff in the council became inspired and came on board to support the project and key community leaders extolled the virtues of the plan. Soon, the press and public were demanding a change and gradually, the expertise I lacked was offered (an architect, an interior designer) and the funding to deliver the project found.

Quite quickly in the process, I became a figure-head for the project and other people took over developing the practical aspects. I learned (and will explain more in Chapter 7: *Energy Intelligent Leaders*), to take my ego out of the venture, to let others receive the praise where it was due. This was alien territory for me as my initial reaction to my hasty promise had been to save my reputation and now it looked like things were going to happen, the 'old me' would have wanted all of the credit for the big risk I'd taken! Instead, I realised I'd moved beyond my old 'ego' self and had worked on the skills and knowledge gaps we lacked to make it a success.

When the library was officially opened, 5,000 visitors attended on the first day. Over the course of the year, library membership was double that of the previous year, issue figures by a similar amount and income from lending CD's and DVD's by 250%! Librarians from across the UK visited our library to see how they could replicate our success.

What I didn't understand at the time was that I had unwittingly found and used Elastic Energy in my workplace.

Elastic energy is the potential mechanical energy stored in a physical system as work is performed to distort its volume or shape. The energy is potential and will be converted into another form of energy for example Kinetic.

My pledge to refurbish the library and the energy and commitment I made, worked to distort its volume and shape. (In fact, we literally did this in a physical sense using floorings, dividing walls and cladding to reduce the vacuous feel of the bowling alley)!

The Potential energy in the staff was released by asking staff to harness their broader work and life skills as well as their professionally trained roles. The use of Elastic energy in the library project was like stretching an elastic band. I put some tension into the team and asked them to do things beyond their capabilities (and the initial resources and support we had). Then, once we'd commenced the project, I let the band go. It flew into the air and landed much further away than the place from which I'd launched it! We now had a challenging target to reach. Our Potential energy was being used. We'd asked 'What Why' and once the project commenced and Kinetic energy was created. The initial force that used power from our own capabilities in the library attracted energy from other council staff and then the wider community.

Somehow, the gap between our resources and aspirations was bridged. The project gained a momentum of its own and we found things were happening with very little effort on our part. We focused intently when we restocked the library and made preparations for the big opening day. After the successful launch, the external environment (in the form of media interest and industry peers in libraries, architecture and engineering) gave us a boost we hadn't envisaged and we continued to find new ways to enable local people to gain benefit from library use. Poole Central Library had built a positive regional reputation!

With Elastic energy, what's interesting is that any force applied to elastic material transfers energy into it. The material then yields its energy into its surroundings and then recovers its original shape. Our 'force' of will and commitment unlocked the Potential energy not just in the staff, but the council as a whole and the wider community to take on the new shape of our aspirations and the library in its new form. Yet, within a year of opening, the original 'shape' was back in place in the sense that, an efficient and effective library service was in operation.

How might this relate to your workplace? If you feel there's enough energy in you and your colleagues to take a 'step-change' in your work, to increase the pace or add to the scope or depth of what you plan to do, you can employ Elastic energy. The first step is to believe that something's possible, even though you don't have a clue how you are going to do it!

The next stage is to decide what the end result will be and then you can work out the gap between what you desire and what you have (in terms of resources, skills and knowledge.)

Hamel and Prahalad's 'strategy as stretch' (11), explains that when your aspiration outstrips your resources and capabilities, a gap is created. The gap is filled by levering in the limited resources and skills available.

By unwittingly applying energy intelligent leadership and encouraging it in my managers and teams, we collectively moved towards our goal step by step with a 'we can do this' attitude and the force of the 'stretch' transferred and shaped us all to be elastic enough to deliver our goal. We delivered a project that was way beyond the original budget offered and our staff capabilities and the project had a far greater impact on the community as we stretched ourselves to go beyond what we thought was possible.

In addition, we sensed our moving up The Energy Spectrum from unhealthy, to average and then to healthy very quickly. The use of Elastic energy made that journey quicker.

Here are examples of individuals who used Elastic energy to create thriving businesses.

Richard Branson is one of Britain's best known and successful entrepreneurs. He set up Virgin Records in 1970, selling via mailorder at discounted prices. "He decided he needed to move to a retail site and persuaded the owners of his first store, above a shoe shop in London's Oxford Street, to let him have it rent free because it would generate more customers for the shoe shop.

It was a great success and he opened up a chain of music stores (later to be known as Virgin Megastores.) Richard next branched into the music business with Virgin Records. Mike Oldfield's enormous hit 'Tubular Bells' was recorded in Virgin's first recording studio – an

Oxfordshire barn – and released in 1973. Other star names signed by Virgin Records included The Rolling Stones, Genesis, Phil Collins, Peter Gabriel, Brian Ferry, Janet Jackson, Culture Club, Simple Minds and The Sex Pistols. In 1992 he sold Virgin Records to Thorn-EMI for almost £500 million."(12)

At each stage of the growth of the business, Richard Branson employed Elastic energy to secure the resources and skills he needed to take the business onto the next level. His positive energy combined with bags of personal style and charm motivated his staff, bringing out their Potential energy.

Even today, it's said he likes to 'keep things small', making decisions face-to-face, keeping his employee relationships personal and informal and seeking out opportunities that fit his longer term goals and aspirations.

He has transferred his energy into sectors as broad as airline, train and space travel to telecommunications and media. Despite the apparent diversification of his businesses, when looked at from the perspective of the Radiant energy spectrum, they fit neatly a long-side each other with clear inter-relationships and have certainly yielded their energy into their external surroundings. Richard Branson has inspired young entrepreneurs to emulate him and has played a role in challenging the establishment over how the lottery, rail and banking franchises are let and run. The business 'empire' is held together by the Virgin brand and the power of Richard Branson's own energy-intelligent leadership style and together; they perform the function of returning the elastic energy's recovery to its original shape.

5 - Radiant Energy

Momentum builds through using the 'other' energies (Rest, Potential, Kinetic, and Elastic) to the point where a state of Hyperfocus is reached. Steve Jobs cut through all the 'guff' at Apple to simplify their business strategy and was a master of Hyperfocus. When all the energies are synchronised, in rare cases, the resulting innovation from Hyperfocus can be so profound, they can change society. This state is called 'energy synchronicity' and from this, Radiant energy is produced. Sir Tim Berners-Lee created energy synchronicity and subsequently Radiant energy with the creation of the internet as did the invention of the steam engine by Thomas Newcomen in 1712 which fuelled the industrial revolution. It is as if something out of nothing has emerged and that 'something' becomes 'everything' in its sector!

You will know when this is about to happen because in your own project when you are aware you have used the appropriate energies and everything is coming together. You are concentrating on what you do and everyone is in Hyperfocus (just as they were in 'The Heart of the Matter'). As I mentioned on page 32, Hyperfocus is where the organisation lights up because it is so focused on something specific and it's going brilliantly.

At this point, Radiant energy will be produced and the brilliance of one area spreads to create dazzling energy in another.

When the mass or system is energised, a reaction takes place where energy is transferred and transformed. Common types of energy transfer and transformation include heating a material, performing mechanical work on it or putting chemicals together to create a reaction. The energy created and carried is called *Radiant Energy*.

Radiant energy is the energy of electromagnetic waves and radiation is emitted by the source into the surrounding environment. In modern applications (solar heating and lighting, telecommunications), it involves transmission of power from one location to another. When this takes place, the mechanism by which energy can leave or enter is known as an 'open system'.

Radiant energy is bright, luminous and resplendent. This energy is so powerful and positive, it transmits itself from one work location to another. It is as if the energy is catching! Creative thoughts are generated into ideas and coincidences abound. Often, one group of staff are developing a product or service at one site and when they share it, they learn important work in the same field is being replicated in another team in the same business! People begin to see these apparent 'coincidences' have a deeper connectivity. It is as if people are joined together by a field of energy that goes beyond the walls of their workplace. In this instance, energy is synchronised and this produces Radiant energy.

There are plenty of examples in the fields of science and the arts where energy synchronicity has happened. One of the most famous is the evolutionary work of Charles Darwin and Alfred Russel Wallace.

"Darwin began formulating his theory of natural selection in the late 1830s but he went on working quietly on it for twenty years. He wanted to amass a wealth of evidence before publicly presenting his idea. During those years he corresponded briefly with Wallace, who was exploring the wildlife of South America and Asia. Wallace supplied Darwin with birds for his studies and decided to seek Darwin's help in publishing his own ideas on evolution. He sent Darwin his theory in 1858, which, to Darwin's shock, nearly replicated Darwin's own."[13]

At the point of energy synchronicity, the release of Radiant energy will move beyond the energy intelligent workplace and out into the wider environment, having a positive impact far beyond the reach of its original intentions and goals.

A similar phenomenon was identified by Charles Handy in his article 'The Age of Unreason', where he states that the invention of the chimney may have caused more social change than anything else!

"Without a chimney everyone had to huddle together in one central place around a fire with a hole in the roof above. The chimney, with its separate flues, made it possible for one dwelling to heat a variety of rooms. Small units could huddle together independently. The cohesion of the tribe in winter slipped away."[14]

Measuring Radiant Energy

The key thing here is that when Radiant energy is working to this degree, *it begins to affect and then change the external environment.* For most workplaces, these wider benefits will be seen as a positive by-product of energy spent. For many, it will be too complicated to measure the long-term impact and benefit back into the workplace. Whilst you won't always be aware of the total impact your workplace is having on the wider environment, you will sense on the far reaches of your awareness, your influence is a positive one. Here are some examples of how the external environment may view your Radiant energy.

✓ Increased brand awareness
✓ You offer value for money

✓ Your products and services are high quality
✓ You offer excellent customer service
✓ A good place to work
✓ An employer with corporate social responsibility
✓ A rise in media attention with positive news reviews and articles

Radiant energy when it's 'out there', is an intangible asset and is worth significant value to your workplace.

David Muir, CEO of WPP *Knowledge Community* states in his paper 'the power of Brands' - "In 1977 intangible asset value were roughly comparable in value to tangible assets. By 2007 intangible assets are worth three times that of tangibles…" (15)

So, once you start producing it, there may well be some merit in spending a bit of energy in measuring the impact of the wider outcomes your Radiant energy produces and you could use the above influences to create measures of performance.

Radiant Energy and the External Environment

The dominant paradigm in management thinking today is that the external environment is unstable and chaotic and that organisations and businesses can do little to change or influence it. There is a sense that any planned strategies will be outdated before they are put into effect and we are buffeted about by the winds of change, completely at their mercy. Workplaces operating Energy Intelligence *can* change the external environment once they generate Radiant energy and this has profound implications for all people who feel unstable in times of rapid change and unable to shape it in any way.

Energy intelligent workplaces producing Radiant energy use less energy and effort gathering and interpreting data, environmental scanning and scenario planning and more energy on energy intelligent interventions. They know they are a positive influence on the external environment and that's all that matters. *How* they impact is less important for they know the benefits will come back into the workplace in ways they couldn't imagine.

In reality, a lot of energy and resources are wasted trying to predict what the external environment will do next. Most of the data gatherers and interpreters never saw the credit crunch coming and it took Queen Elizabeth II (allegedly) to ask for answers to a question most of us had been asking!

"A group of eminent economists has written to the Queen explaining why no one foresaw the timing, extent and severity of the recession.

The three-page missive, which blames "a failure of the collective imagination of many bright people", was sent after the Queen asked, during a visit to the London School of Economics, why no one had predicted the credit crunch.

Signed by LSE professor Tim Besley, a member of the Bank of England monetary policy committee, and the eminent historian of government Peter Hennessy, the letter, a copy of which has been obtained by the Observer, tells of the "psychology of denial" that gripped the financial and political world in the run-up to the crisis." (16)

So, why waste time and resources trying to predict environmental outcomes when 'the professionals' get it wrong? Better to get your own house in order to produce Radiant energy which will have a more long-term stabilising effect on the workplace and the external environment.

Returning back to the Poole Central Library project. Did we create Radiant energy? We were certainly at times in the energetic state of Hyperfocus as for many of us, nothing else really mattered, but had our purposeful work leeched out into the external environment to positive effect? What were the first signs of Radiant energy being produced by the library? I witnessed the first sign of that possibility when I was leaving the library one day for a meeting. It was a week after the new library had opened. A woman stood hesitantly in the entrance.

"Can I help you?" I asked. "What is this place?" she said. "Our new library," I replied. "Is it free to go in?" She faltered. "Come in and I'll get someone to show you around." I answered. I walked with the woman to the joining counter where one of my star library assistants was working. She had a wonderful way with people and was highly emotionally intelligent. She gently led the woman on a personal tour of the library and I watched her relax.

Later, I found out she'd joined and taken out some books to read. Who can gauge what impact this had on her life chances and her quality of life? For many years, libraries have positively influenced our external environment, creating Radiant energy in incalculable ways for so many people.

Too much Radiant Energy?

Even the best solid materials do have elastic limits and beyond this limit, the material isn't able to store all of its energy and the system loses stored internal energy when doing work on its surroundings. So, if you start to get too interested in the effect you are having upon the wider environment and this takes you away from your core vision and goals, you could find your workplace loses energy. It's all about the 'balance of focus'. If you keep energising the internal system, the external environment will benefit and takes care of itself. If your energy is focused too much on the outside, your internal system will weaken. Therefore checking in regularly to see if projects and programmes are still 'on message' with workplace mission, vision and values is crucial. It's also important to check every five years that the workplace doesn't need to alter their mission and vision as well (which will be discussed in detail in the next chapter).

All of the Positive energies I have described in this chapter, form part of The Energy Spectrum. As you apply the strategies described to provide Rest energy and Elastic energy, you will move your workplace up the Spectrum.

Workplaces that use the Five energies are:

- ✓ Clear about their direction and pace of travel
- ✓ Practise Rest energy
- ✓ Utilise some of their Potential energy
- ✓ Clear about the outcomes of projects and the road map for delivering them
- ✓ Harness Kinetic energy

The Five energies will consistently deliver successful high-quality programmes, projects and services. The workplace will be both energised and will operate with energy efficiency and they will stay well above The Stress Energy Tensor, operating in the High Energy Zone. Figure 5 opposite shows the positive and negative energies described.

Fig 5. The Five Energies in Process

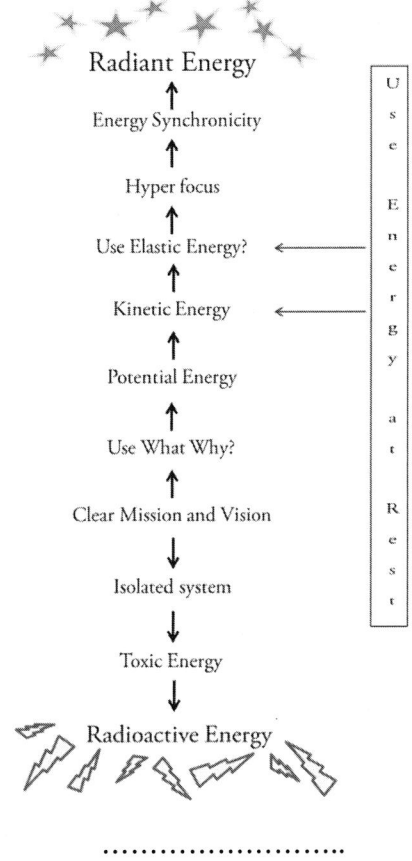

....

Now that you have read Chapter three, here are some Energy Questions to consider:

1. Are there skills that you have which you might use in the workplace (but don't currently)?
   If so, how might you offer these?

2. Do you know of any skills of colleagues that could be 'used'?
3. Might you have more conversations with colleagues about their interests, experiences and skills?
4. Could more be done to identify and harness potential energy within the team and/or organisation? If so – what?
5. Do you build in any periods for rest during the day? What do you do? (it might be a quick stretch, or a walk, or a breath of fresh air…) Are these effective?

Might you do anything differently?

Chapter summary

In this chapter we have explored the range of energies that may be harnessed to aid an organisation's ability to rise through The Energy Spectrum. We are reminded that it is important to create opportunities for Rest in addition to energy expenditure. Potential, Kinetic, Radiant and Elastic energies each offer particular methods by which ENQ can be supported and enhanced, growing motivation and achievement.

In the next chapter we will consider the importance of mission and vision in an organisation, and their primary role in directing activity.

CHAPTER 4

Energy through Mission and Vision

Chapter overview

In this chapter, we learn how workplaces can be energised by a clear mission and vision or conversely, how they can be drained if their 'raison d'être' isn't defined. We learn how to distinguish between a workplace mission and vision and the importance both have in focusing activity and avoiding 'energetic drift'. The necessity for employees to consider whether the mission and vision are in keeping with their own personal beliefs, as well as the potential customer is stressed. Leaders have a vital role in identifying the mission, and in creating, sharing and expanding the workplace vision with managers and teams. Timescale considerations are important within a workplace vision and The Sensory Landscape process is offered as a method that enables leaders and managers to identify themselves and their teams within the vision and the goals that are needed along the way.

These are vital components for the effectiveness of any organisation and must receive regular attention if the application of ENQ approaches are to be effective.

Workplaces that have a clear mission about why they exist and a vision about the direction they are heading towards will be best able to generate energy and control its pace along The Energy Spectrum.

Often, people are confused about what is a mission and a vision, so here's a very simple definition to provide clarity.

Mission: *Your purpose e.g. what you are set up to do.*

Vision: *Where you'd ideally like to be at some point in time in the future.*

Workplaces publish their mission and vision in the form of statements and they can be found on company websites and strategies and are often used to 'sell' the company to existing and potential customers.

Here are some examples of mission and vision statements.

NuYu is a new company providing health and fitness centres for women in Saudi Arabia. It is set up by Sara Al Saud, a leading entrepreneur and business woman.

Vision: "It is our ambition to be the leading provider of fitness facilities for women in the Kingdom of Saudi Arabia. The outcome of which will be a more active, healthier and happier female population who, individually, can enjoy improved levels of fitness and wellbeing and whom, collectively, can make an appropriately positive contribution to the health of the nation."

Mission: "We will achieve our mission by providing licensed, accessible and great value for money venues, which are stylish, welcoming and contemporary in design, where women can affordably benefit from access to the latest training equipment, group exercise activities, expert fitness and nutrition advice provided by international trainers and coaches all in a reputable, safe and supportive social environment." (17)

NuYu are not revising their vision in the medium term as they feel they have got the formula as a whole concept right. To keep on top of the ever evolving fitness industry, NuYu change their programming and classes and alter their resource model accordingly.

Google's mission is: "to organize the world's information and make it universally accessible and useful."[18] There is a company philosophy but no published 'vision statement' about where the company would like to be in the future.

Coca Cola's mission is written in bullet points as follows:

- To refresh the world...
- To inspire moments of optimism and happiness...
- To create value and make a difference.

Their vision statement is: "Our vision serves as the framework for our Roadmap and guides every aspect of our business by describing what we need to accomplish in order to continue achieving sustainable, quality growth

- **People:** Be a great place to work where people are inspired to be the best they can be.
- **Portfolio:** Bring to the world a portfolio of quality beverage brands that anticipate and satisfy people's desires and needs.
- **Partners:** Nurture a winning network of customers and suppliers, together we create mutual, enduring value.
- **Planet:** Be a responsible citizen that makes a difference by helping build and support sustainable communities.
- **Profit:** Maximize long-term return to shareowners while being mindful of our overall responsibilities.

- **Productivity:** Be a highly effective, lean and fast-moving organization." [19]

The BBC's mission statement is: "To enrich people's lives with programmes and services that inform, educate and entertain" and its vision is: "To be the most creative organisation in the world." [20]

Oxfam's mission (written as 'purpose') is "…to help create lasting solutions to the injustice of poverty. We are part of a global movement for change, one that empowers people to create a future that is secure, just, and free from poverty " and its vision "…a just world without poverty. We envision a world in which people can influence decisions which affect their lives, enjoy their rights, and assume their responsibilities as full citizens of a world in which all human beings are valued and treated equally." [21]

People who apply for jobs in companies with clear mission and vision statements should be in no doubt where the interest and focus of their potential employer lies. If their own view doesn't coincide with these statements for example they don't see working for an organisation that prioritises helping people out of poverty as important or valuable, they shouldn't work there!

Many workplace mission and vision statements are unclear for the following reasons:

- The purpose for what they were originally set up to do has changed over time and the mission statement is not representative of who they are today.
- The terms 'mission' and 'vision' are used interchangeably in company publications and is therefore confusing.
- The vision is so aspirational, it can never be attained.

- The vision is realistically attainable but has no time-scale attached, so this lowers motivation and energy.

The vast majority of workplaces never review their mission and vision. Others create theirs as an 'all-things-to-all-people' mishmash. Many in the public sector (e.g. local authorities) fall into this trap because they argue they offer a complex range of services to a cross-section of the public so it's too difficult to pin down what they do. If you look at most council's visions, they are completely interchangeable, even though the population make-up and the geography of their place might be totally different! This is probably because local authority politicians don't like to make too many promises about what's important because there's an opportunity cost somewhere else. If you, the service you run or use are not deemed to be part of the vision and you lose your job or the service closes, you may not vote for the politician who made that decision!

Here are some examples of English local authority visions from north to south, east to west:

a) *"To make ------ a place where all people can thrive; living, learning and working in a clean, safe and healthy environment."*

b) *"------ will be a place where the vulnerable are safe and protected, where employers want to invest and local businesses thrive, and where good health and an excellent quality of life is within the reach of everyone who lives here"*

c) *"To be an organisation of excellence committed to improving the quality of life of all the people of --------."*

d) *"We want to be a vibrant place where every individual and community has the opportunity to grow and reach their potential and play a part in our county's success".*

Broad visions such as these can create what I call 'energetic drift'. What is the destination and in five, ten, or twenty years' time and what will the difference be? If this isn't stated it will be difficult to align policies, plans and programmes.

How can an employee know what's important in their work and what they should be concentrating on first?

Interestingly, I checked to see what the biggest UK public sector employer's vision and mission is. The NHS England's website says in May 2015 our mission is: "High quality care for all, now and for future generations" and its vision: "Everyone has greater control of their health and their wellbeing, supported to live longer, healthier lives by high quality health and care services that are compassionate, inclusive and constantly-improving." [22]

The NHS was created out of the ideal that good healthcare should be available to all, regardless of wealth. When it was launched by the then minister of health, Aneurin Bevan, on July 5 1948, it was based on three core principles:

• that it meets the needs of everyone
• that it be free at the point of delivery
• that it be based on clinical need, not ability to pay [23]

More than sixty years later, it seems timely that the original mission 'good healthcare, available to all, regardless of wealth' should be re-visited and reviewed to reflect society today and the vision of what healthcare will look like in five years' time and how the NHS will get from today to that tomorrow be developed. The five year vision may seem to be a very short time-span for such a huge workplace, but the rate of innovation in medicine is moving so quickly, it's actually a pragmatic thing to do.

In Oxfam's case, to create a 'just world without poverty' might take a little longer!

Energy Intelligent workplaces understand that having a clear mission is crucial because it focuses the attention on the market segment, customer base or type of product or service development i.e. *the business they are in*. In effect, the mission statement defines the territory you are and will be working in for the foreseeable future. As the territory is huge, the workplace is focusing its attention on specific areas so it can deploy its resources and capabilities to best effect.

The workplace vision then becomes both the route map e.g. the journey you plan to take and describes the end destination.

If you were told you could plan a holiday to a country anywhere in the world, you would first think about the places you really want to visit. You settle on one place perhaps because of its wildlife, beaches, city life or because it hosts a festival or you are fascinated by its people. By selecting that country for your own reasons, you are choosing not to explore the territory elsewhere. This is your holiday 'mission', the place and the reasons why you have chosen it.

Next, you do in-depth research, reading about the country you are travelling to. You see pictures of the place, read about its people, their customs and food. In your mind, you conjure up the smells, sights, sounds and experiences you hope to have when you are there.

This is your holiday vision.

Then, you look at your bank balance (I didn't tell you it was a free trip!) and realise you don't have the money to go there. But if you save for a certain amount of time, you can go. If you forgo some meals out, smaller trips and make other economies, you can go on holiday sooner.

You can also choose to fly first class and stay in top hotels, or back pack and fly budget airlines. You can plan to travel by train, hired car or coach when you are there or trek, cycle or 'hitch a ride' to save costs. So, your holiday vision is formed from what you expect or hope the country will be like when you arrive and the travelling experience of getting there.

Who creates the Mission?

The founder members of the business or organisation know why they have set it up and what it will do. Through them, their CEO and leadership team e.g. Board, Cabinet, Directors, are responsible for ensuring that the vision, strategic and operational plans are aligned to their mission. Should the mission change over time e.g. the workplace diversifies into other markets, acquires companies or develops services it is the responsibility of the leader(s) to redefine their mission.

Who creates the Vision?

The Leader(s) should spend time developing a picture of what they want their workplace to be delivering at a specific point in time in the future. They have to immerse themselves in that future as if they were already 'living in it'.

I use a technique I developed called 'Sensory Landscape' and I offer it as a way of helping you place yourself into that future (see below).

The Sensory Landscape Process

Close your eyes and relax. Imagine you are slowly climbing a staircase and that each step is taking you one year into the future. When you have climbed five, ten or even twenty steps, you stop on a gallery to look out at the view.

Next, note everything you see, feel, hear and experience. See what is there, who is doing it, how you feel about that. Note the energy of the place. Who is benefitting and what is missing?

Then, when you have gathered every scrap of information you can find, imagine descending down the stairs year by year until you are back in the present. If you become aware of any activities, scenes, feelings or sounds on that journey back into the present, you can write these down as well.

Fig 6. The Sensory Landscape Process

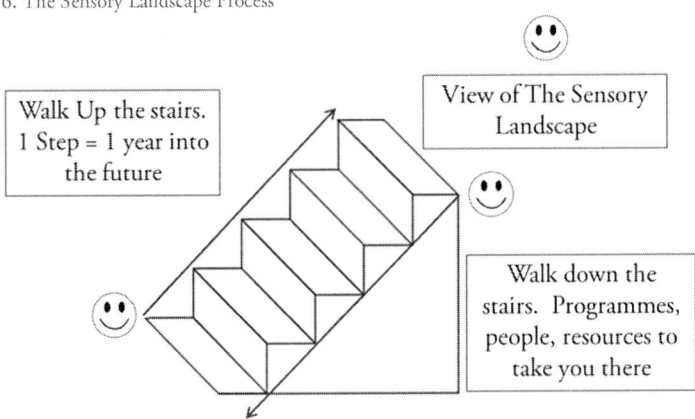

Whilst the sensory landscape may have delivered a vision far and away from the reality of your workplace in the present, it provides you with your desired end destination and a possible route-map for getting there.

The next stage is to share that vision with key managers and teams and have them *discuss it and add to it.* If you are brave enough to take your managers through The Sensory Landscape Process (without telling them your vision first) and have them feedback their experience, there is often a striking degree of consensus with your thinking. This shows you how aligned people are and the likelihood of success there will be.

Managers and teams can become hugely motivated by this process, creating 'mini-visions' for their department and its services. If everyone knows how the product or service is going to operate in the future when it's working at its optimum, then when they look back in time (down the staircase), they can tune things as they go along right back into the present. This can have surprising results as projects deemed important, seen from a fresh perspective, may not be as business critical as others. These 'mini-visions' can be used with my 'What Why' process to apportion resources and guide teams and individuals in their work programmes, leading to a more efficient use of skills, resources and time. In complex workplaces offering a wide range of products and services e.g. local government, a sense of strategic focus will be created under a broader set of workplace objectives.

I was asked to begin negotiations to bring a cinema to a market town. I did my research and contacted cinema owners and CEO's. Having met with them, I was very impressed with REEL Cinemas and its owner Mr. Suri. He told me that he'd always been a keen cinema goer. He felt that some of the large chains didn't reflect the locality they were situated in. For example, they were large anonymous 'boxes' often situated out of town, offering the same food and drink and charging pretty much the same prices regardless of the demographics and economics of the area. His dream was to open a cinema in a town centre that was full of character, offering refreshments suited to the tastes of local people. He also believed that certain groups for example older people should pay less if they came to watch films at off-peak times and he would do a deal (film, sandwich and hot drink) that would be value for money. So his mission was clear (and still underpins everything he does today). On the company website, the mission statement states: "We believe in offering local people a great cinema experience at affordable prices – what we call REEL Value." (24)

Mr. Suri had a vision of owning a small chain of cinemas in towns across the UK within ten years. He knew what they would look like (less screens than a multiplex), friendly very-well trained and motivated staff, offering food for example halal, kosher to reflect local communities and supporting community events e.g. sponsoring cultural activities.

He bought his first cinema in Loughborough - an original art deco auditorium and turned the cinema into an example of his company mission. This was soon followed by others and when senior staff were recruited into the business, it was made clear to them what the company mission and vision were all about. Although REEL has sold a number of its cinemas onto other companies, it has fifteen cinemas in its chain today.

Mr. Suri encapsulates just how a vision should be developed and attained. He set an aspiration into the future for example, to buy a cinema within a year. When he achieved this, he re-set his vision to challenge himself and his team again e.g. to develop six cinemas over a five year period.

Often, when businesses are seeking to win contracts, the difference in the money they offer is marginal. When Mr. Suri came to speak to councillors about developing one in our town, it was his mission of a community space that afforded good value and reflected the needs of local people and the energy and passion of his beliefs that won him the council's support.

He also personally delivered his mission, understanding that the story was his to tell, not to delegate it to anyone else.

If you speak to experienced climbers, they will mostly say that when climbing a difficult peak, the vision is set in 'bite-sized chunks' with enough stretch in them to be a challenge (e.g. reaching base camp,) it provides energy to take them onto the next stage. From then, the next 'vision' may be camp two, then three, then camp four until the summit is reached. Even at that point, surveying a mountain range from the summit makes them realise there are other mountains to climb!

On a similar theme, I set myself the challenge of learning to ski aged forty. My first vision was to imagine myself standing upright on a set of skis and skiing down a gentle incline without falling over. I continued to set mini- visions taking myself forwards in challenging stages until I skied down a black run a few years later!

....

Now that you have read Chapter four, here are some Energy Questions:

1. Are you aware of the mission and vision within your organisation? Try undertaking the Sensory Landscape activity – what are the key issues that arise for you?
2. How does your vision fit with the existing vision in your organisation?
3. As leader – is it satisfactory or is change needed? If so what will be the process and timescale? Will you undertake The Sensory Landscape process with your top team?
4. As manager or individual – how has the mission and vision been communicated to you? Does it have relevance and meaning to you as an individual, to your work? What channels and vehicles are available to you for discussion of this aspect with your organisation?

Chapter summary

In this chapter we explore many issues related to the mission and vision of an organisation. We recognise the importance of the leader in defining and maintaining activity in keeping with its mission, and in creating and exploring organisational vision with managers and teams, adding and expanding where necessary in order to achieve meaningful appreciation and ownership within each team. The Sensory Landscape process helps us place ourselves within the vision and gain a fuller view of the goals along the way. We appreciate the importance of mission and vision in achieving energetic organisational effectiveness.

In the next chapter, we will take a deeper look at motivation and the role of values in defining behaviour within an energy intelligent workplace.

M = Motivation

Chapter overview

This chapter examines the importance of Motivation as a key component of E=MCC. The workplace energy will be significantly increased and easier to manage if staff are motivated. We therefore consider the key elements that make up motivation. We learn the difference between types of motivation and what 'drivers' cause us to be motivated. These drivers are from a baseline level e.g. hunger and thirst to higher levels such as self-determination and actualisation of potential.

Values play a crucial role in an individual's motivation within the workplace. Employees live their life by the values and principles they most cherish; commitment, performance and success at work will be greatly enhanced if personal and organisational values overlap. If work and personal values are in harmony, individuals come to see work as a central part of who they are, what they believe in and how they behave. It is not sufficient for top teams to select organisational values and require compliance and adherence from staff. Teams should be involved in the identification of organisational values, through the 'Ideals Process' which elicits personal values and explores overlap between staff. No more than three values for any organisation are recommended. Once values have been identified and agreed, a wide range of methods to ensure they are 'lived' on a daily basis within the workplace are proposed.

There are many theories about what motivates a person. Abraham Maslow argues in his Hierarchy of Needs'[25], that most people are motivated by unsatisfied needs. The needs start at a basic level and move onto higher desires as follows:

- Physiology (hunger, thirst, sleep, etc.)
- Safety/Security/Shelter/Health
- Belongingness/Love/Friendship
- Self-esteem/Recognition/Achievement
- Self-actualisation

Another theory says that people are intrinsically (internally) or extrinsically (externally) motivated. (26) Intrinsic motivation is driven by an interest or enjoyment in a task *inside the individual* without being motivated by reward or external recognition. When people learn for example, they may do so because they want to master their subject e.g. a martial art or a musical instrument.

Extrinsic motivation comes from *outside the individual.* The activity performed is motivated by rewards e.g. money, passing of exams, or the threat of avoiding punishment. Victor Vroom's Expectancy Theory states that when an employee is completing a task they are influenced by their view on the probability of completing the task and the possible outcome or consequence of completing the task. (27)

My experience of people is that until a point is reached in their lives where they 'have enough' e.g. whatever the individual deems to be enough in material terms, they will be extrinsically driven. Interestingly, the point where material reward is set is significantly lower than people would realise!

According to a recent study on what makes us happy, life satisfaction peaks when income per head reaches £22,000 a year. Beyond this point, we supposedly get richer but less contented and economic growth adds nothing to well-being. (28) The UK has reached this position. A recent Inland Revenue survey, our average weekly pay in

2013, is £517, equating to £26,884 a year before tax and adjustments. (28)

So, if money and external success doesn't always drive motivation, what does? Motivation for most of us is focused on the non-material. We are stimulated by higher desires e.g. a sense of belonging, desiring recognition, obtaining personal mastery and inner growth.

According to 'Self-Determination Theory', people are motivated by a need to grow and obtain personal fulfilment. Note that the theory assumes "...people are actively directed towards this and need to experience three things to be self-determined and in control of themselves and their environment through their behaviours and goals."(29)

The three things fundamental to being self-determined are:

- *Competence:* People need to gain mastery of tasks and learn different skills.
- *Connection or Relatedness:* People need to experience a sense of belonging and attachment to other people.
- *Autonomous:* People need to feel in control of their own behaviours and goals.

Assuming most people will be doing work they are capable of doing, then the other things that keep their motivation focused are a sense of belonging to other people and a feeling of control *over their behaviours and goals.*

We looked at goals in the previous chapter exploring vision and helped you consider ways of setting big goals or visions and mini-goals/visions along the way. In this chapter, we focus on how we can be in control of our behaviour, and collectively, organisational behaviour, through understanding what we believe in and value most in life.

If you know what you believe in and work fits these beliefs, you will become very motivated to realise them, so much so that you will take the external task and internalise it so that you are intrinsically motivated to achieve it. This is the most powerful human driver of all.

The task then is to help you to define what you believe in, what's of critical importance to you personally, so your work becomes meaningful to you. Imagine if most of your work fitted in with your beliefs? How much more motivated would you be? People who are doing work that they believe in are much more likely to be motivated and enjoy doing what they do. My sister is a Doctor. She believes profoundly in saving life and helping people to stay or get well. Her personal belief is improving people's health and fitness. She loves her job and is motivated to work long hours because she believes in what she's doing. Many people don't really know their personal beliefs or find it difficult to articulate them unless put in a position to do so for example being treated unfairly at work makes them realise 'justice' is a personal value!

Workplaces are missing a trick here. If they can help people identify what matters to them and work is aligned to their beliefs, the employee will see the work as being central to who they are and it will become much more important and enjoyable. They will also perform to their highest ability, for by crafting work in this way, individuals are powerfully motivated from the 'inside out' to do the very best they can.

Whilst a clear organisational vision and mission provide a sense of purpose and direction for people, their work has real meaning if it 'fits' with their beliefs systems. Yet, most workplaces don't do work to extract them and then engineer matching work programmes.

What you believe to be most important to you is what you value. Your values define your beliefs and these provide the drive and motivation to live them successfully.

Values and Motivation

In a recent article in Forbes Magazine, a survey by the non-profit organisation *Net Impact* found that fifty eight percent of staff said they would like to work with a company with values like their own.[30] The report cites that values play a major lever in improving employee engagement.

The Guardian newspaper takes the findings one stage further, concluding: "Companies are engaging in these efforts because research shows consumers will pay a premium for socially responsible products, but also because consumers will punish leading firms who fake it. Studies also show that employees consider a firm's values more important than their salary. Clearly, there's solid business reasoning for integrating a values-driven strategy (and living up to it) at your company. But this reasoning is admittedly not unequivocal, or else everyone would be doing it.

So here's one way to think about it: would taking the short-term revenue hit needed to ensure that a company lives up to its values, that staff act in an ethical manner in all facets of the business, and that the firm uses its unique skills and market power to make a difference, pay off for the company?" [31]

If values can make such a difference to people's motivation and to workplace success, what are they?

Values *are the things you believe to be important to you.*

The principles by which people live their lives revolve around what they value. Sometimes, this is easy to identify e.g. having fun is important to me in work (*fun* is the value here), and other times, the value may be deeply important but it is only an ideal to aim for as it's not possible right now. For example Peace is very important to me but I'm working in a warzone right now to help the injured, hoping that one day, peace will prevail (*peace* being the value here.)

Many workplaces have a set of published values and have gone through a corporate process to obtain them; usually the 'top team' undergo a 'word-smithing' exercise where lists of worthy values are written on a flip chart and then weeded-out until half a dozen of the most universally accepted ones are chosen. They are then published and shared with staff.

One business I worked with had fifteen values and asked me to investigate why nobody 'lived' them. I told them to save their money as I could tell them why without asking staff. There were too many to remember and they probably meant nothing to most people as they didn't reflect their personal values! People tend to ignore things they don't believe in or have personal value to them.

My first piece of advice is that no workplace should have more than three values. The reason? *The Rule of Three.* This was developed by Aristotle in his book *Rhetoric* (32) two thousand four hundred years ago and has been used for centuries as a basis for presentation techniques. His theory was that people only remember lists of three things and speechwriters, great presenters and leaders know this. They also know that unless you can repeat these three things over and over, you will forget them!

So, if your workplace has a longer list of values, go back and weed through them until you have a top three!

My second piece of advice is that if your CEO and senior managers develop workplace values and then tell everyone else that's important, it will be like water off a ducks back! This is because the aspiration the leadership team has in any workplace may not be where people are, at the coal-face. It's no good the CEO saying "I want us to value innovation" if teams and individuals are told off every time they try something new or make a mistake.

I was asked to spend time helping a large organisation develop its values. When I took a cross-section of staff through my 'IDEALS' process (more on this later), the values expressed by the top team were very future orientated e.g. *innovate, achieve, aspire*, whilst front line staff were telling me *trust, family, respect* were important to them. I suspected their focus on the present and the behaviours that motivated them may have been driven by a past where the workplace was mistrusting, disrespectful and focused on individuals not teams. If the top team's values had been published as the workplace values, there would have been a major credibility gap within the organisation and the likelihood of these values motivating people would have been very low.

By eliciting values that are genuinely important to people, there will always be a risk that where the workplace is 'at' might not be where its leaders want it to be. If this is the case, a mature conversation needs to take place about what *is* and what is *desired*. In the case where there is a gap between the top team's values and the rest of the workforce, the CEO should have a conversation about the values gap and how it can be bridged. The CEO should also share with staff why his leadership team's values are equally important and valid and discuss what actions should take place to address staff and leader's values.

Before any of this can happen, my two-stage process called IDEALS to draw out workplace values should take place.

The IDEALS process

A sample of at least 15% of all staff from across the organisation should be involved in my IDEALS process. Stage One focuses on gathering individual values and consists of four exercises: *Past, Present, Future* and *Lock-In*. The reason for asking people to work from different time perspectives is that our values change over time. What was important to us, what is significant now and what we might consider to be imperative in the future can be captured and 'locked' together in the present to bring the best of what motivates us in the present with an eye to what might in the future. No matter how uncertain the future is these synthesised values then act as a compass to guide you through life because they give everyone a sense of purpose and direction even if the external environment's values are different.

Stage One

Through facilitated workshops, a cross-section of staff are asked to complete four exercises as follows:

1 - Past

Individuals are asked to think back to a time in work when they were motivated and inspired by their work. They tell a colleague their 'story' and their partner writes down the key values that lie behind their words.

Let's use Fred as an example. "I went to the opening of the building I'd helped to design and build. The project had been a real *challenge* because money was tight, so we had to deliver the brief using our *ingenuity* and *creativity*. What made me really *proud* was we'd introduced *innovations* in the building by taking *ideas* from other sectors and making them work indoors like when we used outdoor lighting in the entrance way because it used bulbs that lasted much longer!

When I saw the *team* waiting for me at the entrance, I was so happy. We'd had so much *fun* working together and they no longer seemed like colleagues, more like *family*! We went in to watch the Mayor cut the ribbon to open the building and I was so *proud* at what we'd *achieved* together."

Fred's story highlights several values which I have put in italics. When you read it again, you may see others and some of them reinforce others e.g. the sense of family, generating ideas, teamwork and working collectively.

2 - Present

Fred is asked to list all the values he believes are important to him in work *right now*. Whenever he gets a 'mental block' and can't list anymore, he's asked to draw a line under his list, wait until he can think of some more values and again, when he hits a mental block, is asked to repeat the process.

Fred's final lists look like this:

Creativity, challenging, ambition, pride, achievement, family, pleasure, happiness, designed

---

Companionship, hope, aspiration, success, together, joy

Adventure, fun, peace, trust, courage

The thinking behind working beyond the lines (that represent mental blocks), is that the first level of values relate to what people believe they *should say*. We are conditioned by our family, society, the media from an early age and we soak up their values like a sponge to the point where we think they are what we value.

Sociologist Morris Massey described how we are conditioned in three major periods during which values are developed.

1. *The Imprint Period.* Up to the age of seven, we are like sponges, absorbing everything around us and accepting much of it as true, especially when it comes from our parents! The critical thing here is to learn a sense of right and wrong, good and bad. This is a human construction which we nevertheless often assume would exist even if we were not here (which is an indication of how deeply imprinted it has become).

2. *The Modelling Period.* Between the ages of eight and thirteen, we copy people, often our parents, but also other people. Rather than blind acceptance, we are trying on things like suit of clothes, to see how they feel. We may be much impressed with religion or our teachers. You may remember being particularly

influenced by junior school teachers who seemed so knowledgeable - maybe even more so than your parents.

3. *The Socialisation Period.* Between 13 and 21, we are very largely influenced by our peers. As we develop as individuals and look for ways to get away from the earlier programming, we naturally turn to people who seem more like us. Other influences at these ages include the media, especially those parts which seem to resonate with the values of our peer groups. (33)

Massey believes by the time we are young adults, the values we acquired in our youth sway what we believe in the present so we are unlikely to challenge ourselves to believe any differently. So my second exercise *Present* reveals in the first and part of the second list values from our conditioning and as the third list emerges, these are likely to be true present values, free from the influence of others. The third level values in *Present* often surprise people because the values expressed are ideals they haven't always done much about, yet they know they are important.

Whilst I've met a few people who have said 'my values never change', most people *do* challenge and re-assess what is of critical importance to them. For example, what was important to me in my early adulthood such as wealth, ambition, success, has become less important as my focus and motivation has shifted towards family, legacy, harmony, even a little fun! Yet, I also know that one value *creativity*, has remained paramount throughout my life so far and I believe it will do so in the future.

3 - Future

Fred is asked to think into the future to the day he retires from work. He is making a speech about all the things he's achieved and talks about the difference he's made. Fred is asked to write this down and when he's read it through, to highlight the values he's described.

"I'm quite embarrassed even imagining making a speech about me to colleagues. I've never wanted to boast about my achievements as I feel I've always *contributed* as a *member of a team*. What I realise though about my career is that I wanted to make the spaces I've designed, places of *beauty*, where people feel *comfortable* and *peaceful* and able to take time out to *relax* from the pressures of work. I'm proud of my *achievements*. Through the *collective* efforts of the *teams* I've worked in, I've left some *innovative* buildings that will be a *legacy* long after I've shifted my mortal coil! I'd like to think that future generations will be *inspired* to think beyond what's possible, to introduce more *ecological innovations* into building design. When I was a boy, I'd sit in my local church built not long after the Normans invaded England. I was *inspired* by how the stonemasons lifted stones to create pillars and arches with only rudimentary tools. I *aspired* to follow in their footsteps and in my own small way, perhaps I've kept that history alive in my craft."

When we place all Fred's values from the three parts *Past, Present* and *Future* together, we get the following values sets:

Challenge, ingenuity, creativity, proud, Innovations, team, fun, family, achieved.

Creativity, challenging, ambition, pride, achievement, family, pleasure, happiness, designed.

Companionship, hope, aspiration, success, together, joy.

100

Adventure, fun, peace, trust, courage.

Contributed, member of a team, beauty, comfortable, peaceful, relax, achievements, collective teams, innovative, legacy, inspired, ecological innovations, inspired, aspired.

Fred is now asked to highlight repeated values from the exercises he's completed *plus any other values that deeply resonate* with him. (This is because once he gets going on the exercises, he may well be reminded of beliefs that are of fundamental importance to him, that for whatever reason, he's forgotten, put to one side or that lay dormant.) His merged set of values becomes:

Team, achievement, innovation, fun, peace, inspire, legacy.

4 - Lock-In

This final part of Stage one in the IDEALS process is to ask Fred to make a choice of his top three values. If he can't decide, he gives each value a mark out of ten (ten being the highest).

Finally Fred gets his top three values: **Team, Innovation, Fun.**

The Individual IDEALS process is shown below.

Fig 7. Individual IDEALS process

Once Fred's and all his other colleagues' individual values have been captured, they need to be assessed, categorised and a workplace values-set produced. This is Stage Two.

Stage Two

This would seem to be an enormous task depending on the size of your workplace, but in practice, you'll find it's not as daunting as it seems!

What you will notice first is how much common ground there is. When you look at all the 'top three' values of staff, many of the values (or very similar ones e.g. group, friendship, community, team) will be shared.

When I did this for a large organisation, I made up a grid and listed the first twenty different values I came across. As I continued to collate all the values from 250 staff, many of them were the same as the top twenty! I ended up finding the same three or four values described in slightly different ways. One hundred and forty five staff listed *trust* (or similar values like *hope* and *faith,*) as one of their values. One hundred and fifty staff had listed *ambition* (or similar values like *aspiration, purpose, drive,*) and eighty six staff had listed *kindness* (or similar values like *care, compassion, considerate*).

So, I offered three workplace values: *trust, ambition* and *kindness.* When they were shared in the workplace, everyone accepted them as they recognised what mattered to them.

This was not a total surprise as the organisation worked in the social care field, so *trust* and *kindness* fitted well. What was interesting is the value *ambition.* It seemed to me that the workplace aspired to do better, perhaps to achieve a specific goal or part of its mission. The three values (known as a 'Values Set') opened up the possibility for some very interesting conversations inside with staff and outside with customers about how these values would be used to treat others, deliver work and explore new services in the future.

Another way of categorising individual values sets is to allocate them under the headings thinking, feeling, creating, believing.

If you consider carefully your workplace mission, you may well find it has subliminally attracted people with certain values.

Google may have people with 'thinking values' e.g. attention, intellect, opinion, detail (with some creating values as well).

Oxfam is likely to have people with 'feeling values' e.g. kindness, caring, helping, sympathetic.

The BBC is likely to have people with 'creating values' e.g. Imagination, aspire, innovative, creative, inventive.

Coca Cola could have people with 'believing values' e.g. harmony, peace, connected, whole, serenity.

If your workplace has had a clear mission-statement operating for some time, people will have already self-selected to join your workplace and in the vast majority of cases, their values will reflect your mission.

You may find you can clump together all the values in one heading into what I call a 'meta-value'. This is the higher power value that encapsulates all of the values in that category as shown in the following example.

- Rational: attention, intellect, opinion, detail.
  The Meta-value is *Balanced.*
- Emotional: kindness, caring, helping, sympathetic.
  The Meta-value is *Compassionate.*
- Creative: Imagination, aspire, innovative, creative, inventive.
  The Meta-Value is *Visionary.*
- Spiritual: harmony, peace, connected, whole, serenity.
  The Meta Value is *Communion.*

You could also choose other ways of categorising individual values sets. You might for example want to look at them by section or team so you can see where there are shared values or if there are maverick values in some areas which could explain why motivation is different across the workplace!

Finally, you may want to consider looking at which values represent what people believe in right now and look at others that may stretch people in the future. If *honesty,* and *respect* are core values held by the staff and leaders/managers have identified their values are *ambition* and *inspiring,* why not start off by living the staffs' values. Once these are embedded in work processes and people are more motivated and confident in the process, introduce the 'future' values of *ambition* and *inspiring* as the main focus a year later? The two future values could provide a motivational stretch for your workplace. You may also decide that a mix of active and passive values works well for you, to stabilise and shift behaviour simultaneously!

Living Your Values

Having gone to so much effort to obtain your core workforce values, how can you use them in work to improve performance, loyalty and openness? Here are some suggestions.

Values Roadshow

The CEO should lead a workplace conversation about what each value *means* so that everyone is clear. This is because we all place different connotations on words. When I use the value *creativity*, I am referring to the ability to think up new ideas. For somebody else, this may mean being artistic or inventing or developing a new design. It's also important to share the values of a similar kind that were discarded in favour of the most commonly used term for example we discarded *aspiration, purpose, drive* and ended up with *ambition*. This doesn't mean the other values aren't important, but this is the one that best describes what's important to everyone. Staff should input their ideas on practical ways to demonstrate workplace values.

Behaviours framework

If you want to change people's behaviour so they apply workplace values to their job, create a Behaviours Framework based on the Values Set you have adopted.

Here's an example for the workplace value *Serve* from an organisation with poor levels of behaviour and motivation who decided to do something about it through the IDEALS process. The meaning behind the value is explained and then staff are given guidance on how they are expected to behave now, and in the future. Leaders and managers should do everything they ask their staff to do as well as having their own set of behaviours!

Once the values have been signed up to by everyone (see opposite), everyone regardless of position has the right to challenge behaviour that doesn't fit the values. For this reason, an explanation of what behaviour will *not* be tolerated in the workplace, is given.

Value: Serve

Definition: Everything we do should be in the best interests of the customer.

Staff expected to:	Staff aspire to:
Listen to customer needs and wants	Identify and communicate improvements to customer service
Provide good customer service	Effectively solve customer problems
Be willing to 'go the extra mile' for our customers	Provide the highest standards of customer service
Value diversity and show respect for all people	Develop and maintain great relationships with our customers

Managers expected to:	Managers aspire to:
Find out what customers need and adapt services accordingly	Identify customer trends, locally and nationally
Set customer care standards for your team to follow	Recognise and reward outstanding customer service
Encourage the team to work together for the benefit of customers	Develop strategies to ensure outstanding customer service
Listen to customer complaints and resolve them effectively and in a timely way	

Unacceptable Behaviour with Serve: You ignore customer's needs, carrying on regardless of what they are saying because you know best! You treat customers differently according to their race, class, sexuality. You know something could be improved but you don't say so. You don't offer help to a colleague when you know the answer to a problem. You don't acknowledge good practice or aren't thanked when you do something well.

Contract of Employment

Every new employee should sign up to the workplace values and behaviours framework and this should be incorporated into their contract of employment.

Disciplinary Procedures

Failing to behave according to workplace values should be included in grievance and disciplinary policies.

Talent Management

More and more people are choosing to commit to workplaces with values like theirs. The Radian Group are a large housing association providing care and support and specialist housing across the south of England. Five years ago, I worked with them to create their values (*Choice, Opportunity* and *Trust*). They are used extensively in corporate information as part of 'Living Your Values'.

Isabelle Simon-Evans, Radian's Director of Corporate Services applied for her job because she was attracted by Radian's values. Talented people are motivated by more than money and by using your values to promote your workplace, this may set you apart from your rivals in attracting the best people.

Reports

Strategies should highlight workplace values and operational plans must explain how the values will be incorporated into internal workstreams and how the values will benefit customers. Projects seeking approval through formal reporting mechanisms should have an 'implications section' for values as well as the usual considerations e.g. financial, legal.

Performance reports should highlight successes and where more work needs to be done in relation to workplace values.

Appraisals

Let's go back to Fred. At appraisal time, Fred is asked to consider by his manager how often he's been living the workplace values and behaviours in his job over the last year and what steps can he take to work with them more fully in the coming year. (He can bring evidence from other colleagues about his behaviour and motivation and so can his manager.) Fred's manager should support him by giving Fred work that suits his personal values to motivate him.

Of course, knowledge is power and should be used wisely, for Fred's manager now also knows that if he wants to de-motivate Fred, he could give him work that is the opposite of what Fred believes is important. In Fred's case, if his manager asks him to work alone, to design and build buildings that are dull and boring inside and out, Fred will be pretty de-motivated and unhappy! Now Fred also has redress. If his manager behaves in this way, Fred can now challenge him directly or through formal processes for not managing him according to workplace values!

Diversity Advantage

There are many studies that prove a diverse workforce has a significant impact on workplace prosperity and creativity. Richard Florida, (Global Research Professor at New York University) says: "To put it in plain English: diversity spurs economic development and homogeneity slows it down.... It's time for diversity's sceptics and naysayers to get over their hang-ups. The evidence is mounting that geographical openness and cultural diversity and tolerance are not by-products but key drivers of economic progress. Proximity, openness and diversity operate alongside technological innovation and human capital as the key engines of economic prosperity. Indeed, one might even go so far as to suggest that they provide the motive force of intellectual, technological, and artistic evolution." (34)

Attracting and recruiting people into your workplace with shared values will improve workplace diversity. If you ask people as part of the application process to explain their personal values and why your workplace values are attractive to them instead of asking them their ethnicity, racial background or sexual orientation, you are likely to end up with a more diverse workforce with shared values rather than the other way round.

I once worked on a cultural project with a man whose family came from India and their family religion was Sikh. In terms of our frames of reference, it would appear we didn't have a lot in common and we may have not connected if we'd just formed opinions on initial impressions. Very quickly, we learned that our families had seen a way to improve their children's life-chances, through a good education, so we'd both studied hard and had been the first in our family to go to university. Our fathers had brought us up with the notion of 'serve not self', so we'd spent part of our careers in the public sector. We both felt our true passion was expressing our creativity, (his through music, mine though developing ideas.) We realised we had deep connections through shared values and we had an amazing time working together. The fear of the 'other' disappeared very quickly and I learned that even though we come from different backgrounds, genders, classes and religions, we could be united in a far more profound way.

Antonym Values

Be mindful that for every positive value, its opposite or antonym exists. For example, the flip-side of *trust* is *mistrust, for ambition* there is *apathy,* for *fun* there is *boredom.* When the values aren't being met in people's behaviours, you may see the opposite values being expressed in frustration.

Mismatched Values

One day, you will find your personal values are not in tune with your workplace, either because its focus and beliefs have changed over the years, or you join a place and find out their values are different to your own. *My advice is to get out as quickly as possible.* If the predominant view of what's important is different and you are in the minority, you will never persuade people to believe in what you do. You are far better finding a place with shared values and until you do, you will be very unhappy and de-motivated.

I was invited by a CEO to find out why his organisation seemed slow to change and to take on board new ideas. His staff, he told me, were 'up for it', but some of his managers did everything they could to hamper progress. I asked if I could hold one to one interviews with the managers he'd mentioned. Having finished five interviews, I realised the average time each manager had worked in that workplace was twenty five years. Nothing wrong with that as their knowledge about the place could have been invaluable. But when I asked them what they believed was important in their work, they shared values like *peace, tranquillity, rest, continuity.* They were frustrated by their CEO and their staff who were pushing them to do things they didn't believe in.

Their values were not aligned to the rest of the workplace who were ambitious, creative and fun-loving. These people were leading people according to their personal values and they were no longer in synchronicity with the majority of the workforce.

My suggestion was that the five managers be given a generous package to leave work and given out-placement support to find work or devote time to activities important to them.

Personal Development Plans

When somebody is considering how to develop their career, I often coach them to look at options from the perspective of their values. This helps define sectors where there is a 'fit'. For example, if you value *wealth* and want to progress though life creating wealth for yourself and others, a business start-up or working in a sector e.g. banking or insurance may be more motivating than working in the voluntary sector. If *care* is a value, then the opposite could be true.

Caffè Nero is a popular European coffee house brand with outlets on most high streets, stations and airports across the UK. The company's ethical approach is: "When we started Caffè Nero, our intention was to cultivate our family feel and grow a business rich with integrity. Now with over 500 stores in the UK alone we continue to take our responsibility to develop a fair and ethical company seriously. We think responsibly for our business and everything we do - how it impacts our local communities, our suppliers, our staff and the environment". (35)

In such companies, the values of family and integrity are often applied even after employees have left the company.

One out-placement job I had with a company that shared these values involved coaching an ex-employee to support her with a career change. When I asked her what truly motivated her, her face lit up and she began talking about her love of animals, especially dogs and cats. She talked about how much she *cared* for them, how *unjustly* animals were treated and how she wanted to *help* them (her values are shown in italics.) When people are truly motivated because they are living their values, you will see it reflected in their body language. They are animated, they move with a lightness of being and find joy in what they do. As she spoke, I could tell she was totally resonant with her beliefs.

Her big dream was to open an animal rescue centre, which was a challenge for she hadn't got a lot of experience in the field.

So we started looking at the small steps she could take to get her to where she wanted to be, fully engaged by what was most important to her. As I described in the previous chapter, she developed a series of 'mini-visions' using the 'Sensory Landscape' process. The first was to work in an animal rescue centre as a volunteer. (If you are already there, when a job comes up, you stand a good chance of getting it). Next, she decided to train in dog grooming so once qualified, she could develop a business and earn money. In the meantime whilst she was studying and volunteering, she decided she was prepared to take paid work e.g. in a bar, restaurant, cleaning, to cover her outgoings. Even if paid work wasn't in the right field, she was earning money to place herself where she wanted to be in the future.

Because she identified what mattered most to her in life, she knew the destination she wanted to arrive at and the stages of the journey required to take her there. Her levels of motivation are high and I know she will succeed.

....

Now that you have read Chapter Five, here are some Energy Questions:

1. Does your organisation state its values? If so, what are they?
   How many are there?
   Can you relate to them?
   How many ways are the values 'lived' within your workplace?
   Are there any activities that do not seem to fit?
   What opportunities do you have for discussion of these issues?
2. What are your own values?
   Try the IDEALS process.
   Is there a fit between your own values and those of the organisation?
3. For leaders and managers. Does any action need to be taken here? Were teams and individuals consulted in their creation? Are they in need of refresh?
   Do teams engage in active engagement with organisational values? Could more be done? If so, what are the plans and timescales?

Chapter summary

In this chapter we have explored what drives people to be motivated (as Motivation is a key element of the Energy Intelligence theory). We learn the importance of values as a central feature of motivation. We have considered use of the 'IDEALS process' to identify a set of organisational values that feel genuine for individual employees since they chime with personal values. Resonance between personal and organisational values ensures colleagues are able to live them in all aspects of workplace activity. We have reviewed a range of methods that can be employed to support this process, ranging from customer service standards to personal appraisals.

In the next chapter, we will explore aspects of commitment for an energy intelligent organisation.

CHAPTER 6

Commitment

Chapter overview

In this chapter the 'CC' in the Energy Intelligence theory E=MCC is explained. Commitment is shown as both a choice and a central component of action for the employee and employer (hence the 'C' 'C' to represent each party).

Drawing on similarities with commitment in emotional relationships, it's suggested that Energy Intelligent organisations would be willing to offer and enact a reciprocal 'commitment contract' which addresses aspects of satisfaction, the quality of alternatives and investments within the relationship. This locks the employer and employee into a mutually-beneficial arrangement. The natural stages within the commitment cycle of foundation, establishment and total commitment are described. It is recognised that such commitments are not suitable for everyone and so exit points within the cycle where necessary are identified. For the majority who do commit, the associated benefits that will be experienced by both the organisation and the individual are great. Both parties become more dedicated to each other as time progresses until a relationship of 'total commitment' is achieved. As with emotional relationships, successful commitment will deepen over time for both parties and the benefits will outweigh the costs of investment.

"Put your head underwater and keep it there for a while.

You'll soon realize that you're 100% committed to breathing.

Notice that you don't make excuses not to breathe. Notice that you don't worry about motivating yourself to breathe. Notice that you don't need to justify your desire to breathe.

115

CHAPTER 6

You just breathe.

Commitment is *action*.

No excuses. No debate. No lengthy analysis. No whining about how hard it is. No worrying about what others might think. No cowardly delays.

Just go.

What if something gets in the way of your commitment?

What would you do if someone tried to prevent you from breathing?" (36)

Knowing what you want to do and believing that you want to do it is one thing. Unless you take action, it's a fantasy, a pipe dream. To commit means to devote time and energy to something you believe in *right here, right now*. Too many people say they are going to commit to something 'tomorrow', 'next week', or 'next month'. Often, it never happens and procrastination takes over. All the reasons why the action hasn't been taken reminds you that the *doing* is all but a pipe dream.

In making an act of commitment, a choice to do something, then other things may have to take a back seat or be stopped all together. I'm not saying it's easy. Once you decide to commit, the focus of your attention shifts away from the past (and all the things you've done that did or didn't work out) and away from the future (and the plans you will enact tomorrow or 'some day') into making a decision in the present.

Think back to times in your life when you made a major commitment, where you signed up to something you believed was important and when you could pledge your complete loyalty. For most of us, these moments are few and far between. The first major commitment I remember making was: 'I promise that I will do my best to do my duty to God, to serve the Queen, to help other people, to keep the Brownie/Guide law.' Whilst the wording of this may be different today, I remember what I said as I joined the Brownies over forty years ago! My commitment was made standing up in front of the whole 'pack' and Brown Owl; a big thing to do when you are nine. My parents had already asked me to commit to other things e.g. go to church on a Sunday, but joining the Brownies was something I wanted to do *for me,* not them. The rest of the time, in my childhood, I made commitments to keep other people happy for example my family, friends, teachers.

As a teenager, I know I committed to a lot of things e.g. playing the piano or to going on a date, but these commitments were easily broken because they were not right for me, or because my attention got diverted onto something else. I committed to things in a hedonistic way because the commitment seemed exciting and it was different or new.

I made short-term commitments where there was an unwritten contract of understanding between me and another party. One example of this was to my teachers at school about homework. They would set it and (most of the time), I would do it because I understood it would help me learn and remember what I'd learned. Homework did not make me devoted to school. I saw it as a means to an end, a contractual obligation that needed to happen so I could stay in school, pass my exams and move on.

It was only as an adult, commitments became more meaningful to me and I stuck with them for longer. Most of these commitments were of a personal rather than work nature. For example, other commitments we might make include being confirmed into a religion, to another person through marriage or civil partnership, or perhaps to a new country of adoption. I also committed to buying a house by signing a mortgage agreement to pay a sum of money every month to my bank until I had paid off the loan I'd borrowed from them.

Sometimes these commitments were made with my head (the mortgage) and others with my heart (taking on two kittens called Pip and Squeak). Very few commitments I've made in my life have involved both head and heart.

I don't recall ever making a major commitment in any job I've ever had and therein lies the problem! Whilst I could make mature, steadfast, commitments to my spiritual, emotional and mental development, I never felt a corresponding obligation to work.

I partially committed to a career in local government because I believed in serving people. So up to a point, the jobs I did offered a fit with some of my values and beliefs, but I always knew I hadn't found my vocation, my life's work, something that I would stick at.

If I'm being really honest, I did my job as well as I could but I always felt restless, hoping there was something better coming round the corner. I was self-motivated and could be motivated with like-minded colleagues, but felt that beyond this, I was working in a vacuum. I wasn't committed to my organisation because I didn't believe in its leaders, the ability of all of us to control our own destiny and to shape the future without massive interference from external factors e.g. government policy. The 'push-pull', 'start-stop' of projects and activities that were the next best thing and then abandoned after a lot of effort, switched on and off my levels of dedication and loyalty until I became indifferent.

If we can make a long-term commitment to things outside of work, why can't we do it in work? I'm not aware of many examples where people make a heart and head commitment to their work. Doctors and healthcare professionals make the Hippocratic Oath; "I will use treatments for the benefit of the ill in accordance with my ability and my judgment, but from what is to their harm and injustice I will keep them".(37) The legal profession signs an oath of office and there has recently been some debate as to whether lawyers and barristers should have an equivalent Hippocratic Oath for their profession. Presidents and Prime Ministers are sworn into office.

Apart from the Hippocratic Oath sworn by the medical profession, most pledges are asking people to agree to an ethical framework. Whilst a promise is a promise, it may be seen as an obligation or a hoop that needs to be stepped through, rather than a commitment that will bring dedication, loyalty and devotion.

The form of commitment we should be making if we are to enter the world of Energy Intelligence is similar to that made in a romantic partnership, whereby two parties come together to promise to respect and support each other on a range of things important to them e.g. financial, emotional, mental. Over time, as these pledges are delivered upon, the parties become more dedicated and loyal to the relationship and this develops into devotion and steadfastness.

Caryl Rusbult (38) developed the *Investment Model of Commitment Processes* to predict levels of commitment in romantic relationships.

Three factors influence relationship stability:

1. *Satisfaction*: The individual believes the relationship is rewarding e.g. there is good social and financial support, shared interests, sexual gratification and low conflict and irritation.
2. *Quality of Alternatives*: The individual looks at the rewards and costs that could be obtained outside the current relationship e.g. a new relationship, spending more time alone or with friends and family and believes it wouldn't improve the overall quality of what they currently have.
3. *Investments*: The individual weighs up the time, money and investment they have in the relationship and what they would lose if it were to end.

People in relationships who have high satisfaction and investment levels and low quality of alternatives levels will be committed. The longer the commitment remains, the more stable the relationship becomes.

If we look at how this model could relate to your workplace, (I'm not suggesting that sexual or romantic gratification is a pre-requisite for making this a success…), the individual has to feel work is rewarding, the quality of what's on offer in other workplaces is inferior and the investment made in them and by them is substantial and will be hard to improve. So, Rusbult's Model is modified to fit the workplace as the *Commitment Contract*.

The Commitment Contract

Workplace leader and managers should think carefully about what they can offer as employers to employees as a 'sign' of their commitment. For example:

Satisfaction

Pay and associated rewards are at least at the industry average if not higher. There are clear paths for progression for people who perform well and opportunities for learning and development to gain promotion and/or advance professionally. If the workplace performs well, all employees who have made a positive contribution should be equally rewarded (e.g. in the form of a bonus, shares, additional annual leave, meal vouchers as appropriate.) Other forms of support to increase individual satisfaction could include organised social events, health and well-being initiatives such as health checks, reduced gym membership and the opportunity to try out a new hobby or activity. Policies offering a healthy work-life balance with good leave entitlement, working hours and friendly childcare policies will also improve overall satisfaction.

In case there is conflict, a clear process for reporting issues and problems should be in place and should be able to demonstrate conflict resolution. (There's nothing worse than knowing if you complain about someone or something or whistle-blow, nothing gets done about it.)

They should also ensure that employees are satisfied, they know what is going on in the workplace through high quality internal communications processes and that managers are playing a key role in supporting and developing staff and managing their performance.

Employee satisfaction can be measured through regular employee engagement surveys, through leaders 'walking the floor' and providing a range of opportunities to give views, ideas and feedback.

Quality of Alternatives

The employee knows that they are so satisfied by the personal opportunities offered by their workplace that when they look elsewhere, nothing really matches up to the totality of what they currently have. For example, they could get a better paid job, but not have the training or social opportunities; or a new job would give them a promotion but it would be at the cost of a healthy work-life balance. The individual looks at the rewards and costs that could be obtained outside the current arrangement e.g. a new personal relationship, spending more time alone or with friends and family and believes it wouldn't improve the overall quality of what they currently have.

Investments

The employee recalls all of the costs the workplace has made in their training and development and all the employee social care programmes they have used. They also think about the work-life balance (the times they have been given support through ill health or caring for family), annual leave and other benefits and will be adding in the value of this to their salary and potential earnings, promotion opportunities and possible future training support.

The employer is aware of the investment in time and money in the employee's recruitment, development and the cost of replacing the employee's knowledge, skills and experience were they to leave.

In addition to the above, there are some 'soft commitments' employers and employees should promise to each other. For example, the employer should provide clear guidance on the behaviours expected to support the delivery of company mission, vision and values and to manage the energy of the workplace. The employee should promise to behave in ways that support their delivery.

The above 'rights' for employees should come with corresponding 'responsibilities'. Rather than reducing commitment, I believe this increases it by placing an equally important and valued set of obligations on the individual and the employer.

So, the employee should pledge the following commitments:

- Keep focusing on their work goals even when things aren't going well in the short-term.
- Stick with the long-term vision of the workplace.
- Express when they are feeling de-motivated and why and offer solutions and ideas to resolve the problem.
- Avoid quick fixes or going off plan for short-term gains.
- Live workplace values and behaviours to the best of their ability.
- Both parties must take full responsibility to ensure the commitment process is maintained (hence the 'CC' in my Energy Intelligence Theory).
- Share their skills and experience widely in the workplace. Energy Intelligent employers and employees are prepared to make a significant commitment to each other knowing that in doing so, they are adding value to the E=MCC theory.

The Stages of Commitment is outlined in figure 8 overleaf and consists of three stages resulting in Total Commitment.

Stage One - Commitment Contract

An initial commitment is made by the employer and employee when an offer of a job is accepted. This should be an important rite of passage into the workplace for all new employees via a practical induction into the workplace called the Workplace Induction programme (WIP).

The WIP is a homophone, a word that has the same sound as another word (whip) but is spelled differently and has a TOTALLY different meaning!! The WIP should offer workshops on workplace mission, vision, values, duty of care, strategic and operational plans and how the new employees can contribute to them. There should also be Energy Intelligence classes to introduce the concept.

Assuming they have been inspired and excited by the WIP, the employee is given a Commitment Contract to sign before beginning work.

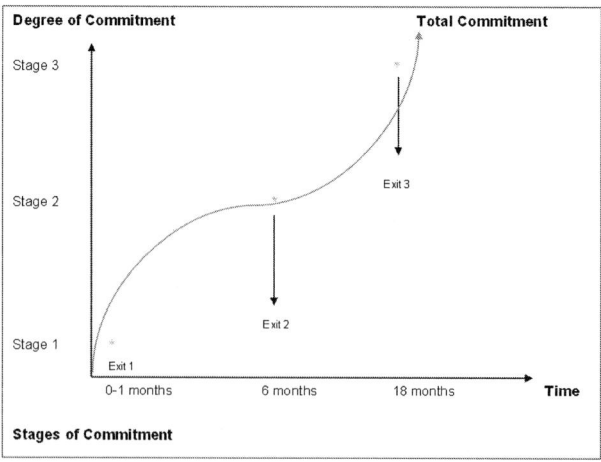

Fig 8 Stages of Commitment

The Commitment Contract is so much more than an employment contract, for in addition to the elements I mentioned on page 121 and 122, the contract outlines *the way* the organisation does things, what the employee can expect and what's expected of them.

The Commitment Contract acts as a bonding agent between employer and employee and employee to employee. It gives a sense of 'esprit du corps'; that 'we are all in this together'. It is the first step in a process that leads to 'total commitment' which will happen when the pledges that have been made are consistently delivered over time.

It would be great if a Commitment Ceremony is made, perhaps between the CEO and the employee at this stage in the commitment process to show that the obligation is equally met by both parties.

Stage One Exit 0-1 month

Having attended the WIP, the employee can turn down their offer of employment and the signing of the Commitment Contract if they don't want to invest in the workplace further.

Stage Two - Foundation 0-6 months

During Stage two, the employee will be judging (according to their perspective and the evidence they find) whether the employer is living up to 'their side of the bargain'. Similarly, the employer will be checking the employee's behaviour and their actions fit in with workplace values and behaviours. Stage two is like a probationary period which lasts up to six months.

Not all relationships run smoothly and at times, there will be 'ups and downs'. For example, the employee might try to challenge or test the workplace culture by keeping information to themselves. They may find the new mind sets and behaviours a challenge. They may find they are joining at a time when elastic energy is being employed and they are expected to work to a goal without all the resources and capabilities they need. Or, they could be joining after a large programme has been successfully implemented and the workplace is 'at rest' when they want to go full-steam ahead.

Working in an Energy Intelligent organisation will lead to new experiences and some surprises that can be both positive and negative. The onus here is on the employer to allow the employee to 'test' and 'be tested'.

Stage Two Exit at 6 months

At this stage, either party can end the probationary period. After six months in the workplace, the employee should have a detailed appraisal with the employer. This should involve a mature and open discussion on all elements of the Commitment Contract and whether its terms have been realised. Where there are areas of concern, every effort should be made to solve problems, encourage action to take place and build accountability. Despite the obstacles and challenges, if the employee has demonstrated they've maintained their commitment, more support is then given (in the form of additional resources and rewards).

The Foundation Stage is designed to develop a joint conviction through promises and assurances that the employee is becoming loyal to the workplace.

Stage Three - Establishment 12-18 months

This is the time where the 'Foundation' period has been completed and approved and the employee 'beds down'. They are now established in the workplace, and starting to deliver high quality work and behaviours.

The employee feels valued, is able to work creatively and imaginatively with support from their manager and leader where appropriate. Morale and motivation is high in individuals and teams and work is progressing successfully. The employee understands and supports organisational changes. What results is a standard way of operating and the employee becomes an energetic contributor to the workplace. A personal choice to remain and dedicate oneself to the workplace is made. Recognition in the form of increased employee benefits should be awarded by the employer and employees passing through 'Establishment' should have this commitment publically announced to and celebrated by all colleagues. Existing employees should pledge to honour workplace values. (I don't want to be over-the-top here, but if you think about it, you are only asked to make a pledge a few times in your life. So for many people, this has meaning and significance. You may have made a pledge when you joined the Guides or Scouts, admitted into your religion, when you married or entered into a civil partnership. Your workplace could make this a really significant and important right-of-passage into being 'one of us'!)

Stage Three Exit at 18 months

At this stage, some of the more deeply hidden cultural norms may become apparent. For example, subtle political influences within teams, systems or logistics that work in theory but not in practice and changes that take place that don't fit with the individual.

It's possible that an employee will conform to workplace norms but will only mimic desired behaviours. This can be for a number of reasons for example the investment they have made, the alternative jobs in their sector being poorer, their beliefs being different to workplace values. On-going dialogue and observations from managers and colleagues through 360 feedback (a process that includes direct feedback from an employee's subordinates, peers, colleagues, and supervisor(s), as well as a self-evaluation. It can also include feedback from customers, suppliers and other interested stakeholders). This will establish whether their actions are aligned to workplace expectations and norms.

The Commitment Contract can be broken by either party at this point if allegiance on either side is wavering or 'half-hearted'. The employee should be given a generous severance package with outplacement support. I argue this because the cost of poor employee relations, reduced productivity and increased resources used in resolving these issues, may far outweigh any severance payment made to the individual concerned.

Total Commitment

This is the final stage. Total Commitment represents the highest level of dedication and loyalty to the workplace. The employee exhibits high levels of intrinsic motivation and is fully aligned to the workplace mission and vision. Their individual beliefs and desires are aligned and consistent with workplace values and behaviours. Employees are to a large degree self-managed and demonstrate in their work, high levels of personal responsibility and accountability, doing their very best to make a success of everything they do.

They act as champions and advocates for their workplace in the external environment and they protect and build workplace reputation. They are energised and energetic, suggesting ways of improving existing processes, systems, products and services, acting as a mini 'think-tank' of ideas and suggestions.

Rewards continue to accrue for both parties reflecting dedication to work and allegiance to the workplace. Employees who are totally committed have a senior sponsor who guides their progress through the workplace. The sponsor should act as a coach and mentor to the employee and should not line-manage them. The Sponsor should be empowered by the leader to be open to making adjustments to and learn from the employee. They are there to help foster change in the employee and be prepared to change and adapt their way of thinking and behaving. Sponsor and employee can discuss new forms of mutual commitment and the potential rewards that will accrue which could lead to transformational change for the employer and employee. These new commitments get fed into work objectives for the coming year and are shared with line managers. The overall aim of this is 'to persist to commit.' Total Commitment therefore energises both the employer and employee, moving them towards new horizons on what can be achieved and how it can be delivered. The process leading to Total Commitment unleashes positive energy and allows it to flood around the workplace and removes the uncommitted with their negative energy from it.

Employer and employee will move around the Total Commitment cycle (see fig. 9 overleaf) depending on their understanding of what is required of them at a fundamental level related to values, beliefs and individual choice. Over time, the commitment deepens as parties resolve to continue their mutual support. The life-span of the process continues until the employee leaves or retires.

Fig 9. Total Commitment

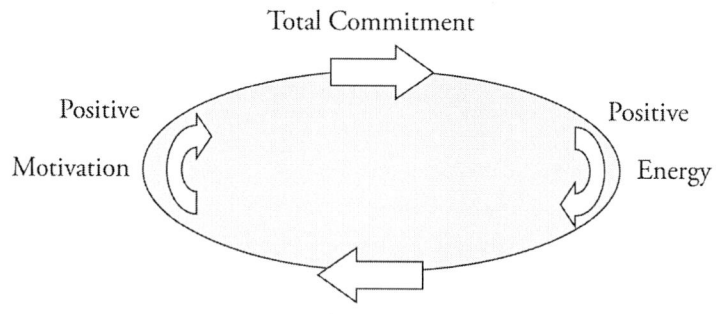

Cost of Commitment

Time and money will need to be invested upfront and during this process. Investment will feature most in creating robust commitment strategies, induction programmes and the Commitment Contract as well as rewarding employees for passing through the three Commitment Stages. Costs are also associated for removing the 'uncommitted' from the workplace.

The benefits accrued will far outweigh the investment made. Energy Intelligent organisations who aim for Total Commitment, will be rewarded with faithful, steadfast and loyal employees who are dedicated to the workplace and their work. Over the medium term, retention rates will be high, sickness and recruitment rates low and knowledge and talent will stay in the workplace to generate fresh ways of thinking, new ideas and innovation in services and products. The value externally of employees acting as champions will add value to the workplace brand and raise its standing as an enlightened employer. The consequences of not doing so are far higher!

A quick mention about 'commitment phobes'. There are many people who don't want to commit to anything, let alone work. They have a different view of the world (which I explain more in Chapter 10 *Energy and Time*) which is based on a Present Hedonistic time perspective. In Energy Intelligence, commitment is a major component of success for individuals and workplaces. So, the simple truth is, if you don't want to commit, that's fine, but don't work in an Energy Intelligent workplace. If you lead an Energy Intelligent organisation, don't take on people not committed to workplace vision, mission, values and all that goes with them.

....

Now that you have read Chapter six, here are some Energy Questions:

1. Does your organisation have a 'Commitment Contract'?
2. If it does, how does it work? Might it be in need of attention, refresh? Is it a real and active process, or is it merely lip-service? What are the benefits? Could these be strengthened?
3. If there is no contract, could it be possible to introduce the concept? What might be the benefits to your organisation? What could the process look like for induction?

Chapter summary

In this chapter we have identified the importance of commitment in relationships. We have drawn parallels between emotional and workplace commitments, recognising that an energetically intelligent organisation will engage with employees in a 'Commitment Contract'. The process and timescale are described here. We recognise that the commitment will grow stronger over time, with benefits far outweighing costs, being energising for both parties. In the next chapter we will explore the qualities and characteristics of Energy Intelligent leaders.

CHAPTER 7

Energy Intelligent Leaders

Chapter overview

In this chapter 'The Baker's Dozen' features of the Energy Intelligent leader are identified. These are quite different in several respects from the usual list of skills and attributes that one might see in other literature. Some will be expected of course, such as 'setting the direction' and 'aligning values', though others will be less familiar such as 'observing the flow', and I hope that a few will be quite surprising such as 'asking Bob' and 'being a time lord'! Try to keep an open mind and engage with these as fully as you can.

The energy questions at the end of the chapter will help you review yourself in relation to The Baker's Dozen, and to set appropriate goals and timescales for action if change is needed.

The Baker's Dozen

Energy Intelligent leadership requires a very different set of skills, style and behaviours from those we have been used to in the twentieth and early twenty first century. The Energy Intelligent leader has to possess a high level of Energy Intelligence (ENQ), to be able to create with others high motivation and commitment and to regulate the flow of energy in the workplace. If you re-read 'the Heart of the Matter' on page 19 and then see how the leader handles things on page 20, you'll realise there are some clear characteristics, functions and competencies specific to energy intelligent leadership. I call these 'The Baker's Dozen'.

133

1 - Set the Direction

The role of an Energy Intelligent leader is to act as a catalyst to 'get the mass moving', to set the direction for the workplace through a clear mission and a succinct vision. If the existence of the workplace pre-dates the leader, it may have a historic mission and vision that is no longer fit for purpose. The leader's core function is to review these with the support of the workplace governing body and to take the workplace through the Sensory Landscape and IDEALS processes I outline in Chapter 4 *Mission and Vision.*

This is an essential piece of work because Energy Intelligence can only expand if individual staff are committed to the workplace vision and mission.

These are necessities that cannot be delegated and **can only be led by the CEO**. As the workplace leader, it is vital they know what they are trying to do and can explain this to employees and stakeholders. As Peter Drucker said; "Leaders communicate in the sense that people around them know what they are trying to do. They are purpose-driven-yes, mission driven. They know how to establish a mission." (39)

In *The Heart of the Matter* (page 19-20), the leader knows this team is 'doing the right thing'; that they are fulfilling their mission and purpose within a defined time-scale. In this case, the workplace mission is 'to save life' and the vision is to carry out six successful heart transplants a year with 85% of patients alive and improving three years after the operation.

Getting this cornerstone laid firmly in place is the core function of the Energy Intelligent Leader and if they can do this in the simplest and clearest way, so much the better! The leader should be regularly asking; *"what business are we in and what do we want to achieve over a three, five, ten, twenty year period?"*

Leaders can use *Set the Direction* to benefit a wide range of workplace initiatives. For example, they can say no to anything that doesn't fit the core mission and vision. For example, when recruiting staff, the workplace can say "this is who we are and we are passionate about *this*. Don't come here if you don't like this or think you can change us from the inside out."

A retired University Vice-Chancellor told me that when he was involved in senior staff recruitment, he always made it clear to applicants his university mission was to provide an excellent education for the disadvantaged and his vision was to encourage young people from ethnic minority and low-waged family backgrounds to study for a degree. The staff in that university were motivated and committed to working to this ambition and the policies and procedures were aligned in support. An academic applying for a position in this university who didn't share the same mission and vision was under no illusion this wouldn't be the right place for them and anyone who was already working there who tried to resist or change things wasted a lot of energy and ultimately left for a University with a different focus.

2 - Align Values

It's also vital that the *way* the company operates e.g. its values and beliefs are set out clearly. The Chief Executive or Managing Director will want to review all of these and should engage all the existing staff in the process I outline in Chapter 5 *Motivation*. Clarity on workplace values and the behaviours expected to realise them will ensure employees are motivated to perform because their values and beliefs are shared and aligned.

As I mentioned on page 107, Radian is a large housing association and care provider in the south of England. It has gone through a significant transformation over the last five years. When three housing associations merged to form Radian, it was beset with behavioural challenges. The three housing associations had very different values. One for example, acted like a 'family' (which was fine if you were a 'relative', but not so good if you were a 'stranger'). Like most families, behaviour when functional revealed a close-knit community of staff who cared, and when dysfunctional, there were falling outs and an inability to integrate with others 'not like them'. Other areas of the organisation were far more commercial in their outlook, others more service driven. Quite naturally, people were uncertain about the motives of others in the group, where they would be in the 'pecking order' and behaviour now deemed as unacceptable was tolerated because there wasn't a clear set of expectations on how to act.

Lindsay Todd, its new Chief Executive, recognised that a set of organisational values would underpin the mission and vision he was creating for Radian and would signal to employees the principals and standards of behaviour expected.

Radian's values *Choice, Opportunity, Trust* were created by the leadership team and staff. Lindsay Todd took personal ownership of the values, committing himself to road-shows where he personally explained how he would like the values interpreted by employees in the way they behaved towards each other and their customers. Over time, Radian's values have been underpinned by a behaviours framework and are used on all promotional materials including staff recruitment and performance management.

3 - Decide and Stick

In *The Heart of the Matter,* the leader makes the key decision that commits everyone to a course of action (i.e. to collect a heart and transplant it successfully). An energetic response is thus created. The staff spring into action. Once the choice has been made, she doesn't alter it. Her role is to make the decision and then trust her manager to support the team to do its work. Her role is complete for now. She will not hamper or constrain them in any way. In fact, she isn't a heart surgeon. She has people in her workplace who are far better at this work and the many other things that support the process. She's learned to let them do the work they were trained to do. Her role and experience is in Energy Intelligent leadership and to back off to let others do their job. That's what she does best and directs her energy and focus towards leading.

Leaders with a high ENQ know that leadership is about making the big decisions. Craig Richardson, Managing Director of Wynyard Group, and former CFO of Coca-Cola Amatil's Pacific operations says *"The fact that as CEO you must make the big decisions, and live or die by them. Once you are the CEO, all those decisions sit with you. This includes making complicated judgment calls, even when there is a lack of data. You have to have a high level of confidence that you can live by the decisions that you make."*(40)

Quite often, the decisions that need to be made are complex and costly to the workplace. Better to have a leader who does nothing but spend their time making the right decision than working on other things and paying half the attention needed on what is business critical.

Energy Intelligent leaders who focus on *Decide and Stick* are akin to diamond cutters. To cut a diamond and grind fifty seven facets at precise angles takes many years of experience and the job cannot be rushed. Make a cut or grind in the wrong place and the stone is virtually worthless. With large, valuable, diamonds, the process can take a long time. It would appear that not much progress is being made with all the observing and sitting around, but that is an important part of the process of getting it right for the costs of not doing so are great!

I would go as far as to say that the leader is paid to take big decisions and shouldn't do more than two 'pet projects' on top of this in a year. The rest of the time, they should be focused on the 'Baker's Dozen'. They should keep away from meddling with everything else because there are accountants, lawyers, managers and staff to do this for them. There's only one CEO and their time and energy focus needs to be on Energy Intelligent leadership!

---

4 - Leave well alone

My experience of working with many leaders is that *they just can't leave things alone*. With the best of intentions, they meddle, get in the way and even worse, half way through a project, programme or activity, they change their minds and change direction. Everybody on the receiving end of this indecision is muddled and irritated (and probably resigned to the fact it's 'here we go again'). As I explained in Fig 3 the Energy Spectrum (page 35) and Fig 4 the Stress Energy Tensor (page 36), the lack of clarity around strategic priorities and 'drift' away from workplace vision and mission causes 'force-fields' to emerge within individuals and teams. People are doing too many things and none of them well.

Because workplace aims are unclear, staff place their own interpretation on what they think is important. Instead of people operating freely within one coherent strategic force-field, many smaller fields are created that chafe against each other. Performance drops and energy levels begin their downward spiral. If the leader *Decides and Sticks* and then *Leaves Well Alone*, people are clear about their objectives and are trusted to get on with them and do them well. This is a motivational leadership act and enables the workplace to move up the Energy Spectrum to produce Radiant energy.

I recently had the privilege of facilitating a leadership conference where the guest speaker was Christian Gansch, the great classical music conductor. In his inspirational speech on leadership, (where he used his experiences of conducting an orchestra), amongst many of his excellent examples, one particularly struck a chord (pardon the pun)!

He said that when a musician (let's say a flautist) was about to play a solo, the last thing he would do would be to conduct them. In his view, that person had trained in the best music schools to gain a place in the orchestra. They were qualified to play the piece to a high standard and if he made a dramatic intervention, it would be at best off-putting and at worst a total intrusion. It would imply he had no confidence in the flautist's ability or professionalism.

Mr. Gansch chose to leave the flautist well alone to concentrate and play her solo. He gently marked the rhythm whilst the soloist played her part 'radiantly' and directed his energy to bringing in the rest of the orchestra as appropriate.

5 - Praise and Commemorate

In *The Heart of the Matter* on pages 19 and 20, the Leader waited for the result and was ready to celebrate it when it came in on time and to budget. The ENQ leader gives credit where it is due and praises and rewards when appropriate.

Dale Carnegie wrote 'How to Win Friends and Influence People in 1937. His sixth principle of *Be a Leader* is "Praise the slightest improvement and praise every improvement. Be hearty in your approbation and lavish in your praise."[41] Over seventy five years later, this still holds true and lots of employee surveys including the one below from the USA, tell the same story.

"The online jobs and career community Glassdoor just released its Employee Appreciation Survey, revealing how appreciated employees feel by employers, what really motivates them at work and what employer-provided perks they want most this Thanksgiving.

The survey, conducted online by Harris Interactive on behalf of Glassdoor among 2,044 workers, found that 53% of employees would stay at their company longer if they felt more appreciation from their boss. In addition, 81% said they're motivated to work harder when their boss shows appreciation for their work.

"This Glassdoor survey is important because it reminds employers of any size that you don't need fancy perks or a big budget to retain talented workers," says Allyson Willoughby, Glassdoor's senior vice president of people and general counsel. "In fact, this survey shows that most employees just want to feel appreciated and valued. They want to be involved in decision making processes, do interesting work and have a purpose. If employers keep this in mind, they'll likely longer retain some of their most talented employees." And don't forget, she says, "the time a boss spends showing some appreciation, thus helping retention, is time spent not having to recruit and interview an employee's replacement." (42)

Knowing what is going well in your workplace means 'walking the floor', talking to managers and staff. You cannot do this if you are tied to your computer sending out e-mails. Leaders should apportion at least one fifth of their working week to 'nose out success' and a simple thank you or an invitation to your office to give praise over coffee, will make employees feel valued, motivated and energised.

6 - Carry the Can

The Heart of the Matter leader 'carries the can'. Had there been problems, she would have been ready to support her managers to help iron out any problems. If her judgment had been wrong, she would have taken full responsibility for her decision. The blame would have been shouldered by her alone.

So often these days, when mistakes are made or wrongdoing done by people in positions of authority (politicians, the police, civil servants, hospital staff), they blame everybody but themselves. I'm not asking leaders to fall on their swords every time something goes wrong. Mistakes happen and a leader can't always know everything that's going on in detail in their workplace. But they can and should be aware of where energy changes and that sense should set them on a course of action to find out why or what is happening. To deny all knowledge or to obfuscate is to not be responsible when you hold the ultimate position of accountability and are being paid to do so.

Energy Intelligent leaders should 'own up' as soon as the problem comes to light and explain what they and their colleagues are going to do about it. After all, they set the standards of behaviour and should be seen to be living them. Usually, that's enough to maintain the trust and respect of staff and customers. When errors are made time after time and the leader doesn't take responsibility resulting in action, employee motivation and energy lowers. It is at this point that the leader should consider their position.

7 - Set the Velocity

The leader needs to be mindful of keeping the workplace above The Stress Energy Tensor and should have a series of strategies in place to keep energy levels high, but not so high that staff become stressed and eventually radioactive. Neither should the pace be too slow so potential energy lies dormant.

I have seen and used myself the tactic of creating energy by saying there's a problem or 'crisis' that needs to be sorted quickly when I've noticed people are 'off the pace'. Occasionally, I've developed a 'vision' of alternate possibilities or scenarios to shift people to deliver. The only problem with this is by 'conjuring up' either in the short-term, it's not the most authentic thing to do. It's a form of cheating and makes a mockery of having a solid mission and vision and is incongruent with the values and behaviours expected of an Energy Intelligent leader. In the short-term, people will follow the leader to get the job done but they know they have been 'played' and it makes them more wary when the same kind of thing is asked of them further down the line. It becomes a case of the 'Boy Who Cried Wolf' in Aesop's Fables.

"There once was a shepherd boy who was bored as he sat on the hillside watching the village sheep. To amuse himself he took a great breath and sang out, "Wolf! Wolf! The Wolf is chasing the sheep!"

The villagers came running up the hill to help the boy drive the wolf away. But when they arrived at the top of the hill, they found no wolf. The boy laughed at the sight of their angry faces.

"Don't cry 'wolf', shepherd boy," said the villagers, "when there's no wolf!" They went grumbling back down the hill.

Later, the boy sang out again, "Wolf! Wolf! The wolf is chasing the sheep!" To his naughty delight, he watched the villagers run up the hill to help him drive the wolf away.

When the villagers saw no wolf they sternly said, "Save your frightened song for when there is really something wrong! Don't cry 'wolf' when there is NO wolf!"

But the boy just grinned and watched them go grumbling down the hill once more.

Later, he saw a REAL wolf prowling about his flock. Alarmed, he leaped to his feet and sang out as loudly as he could, "Wolf! Wolf!"

But the villagers thought he was trying to fool them again, and so they didn't come.

At sunset, everyone wondered why the shepherd boy hadn't returned to the village with their sheep. They went up the hill to find the boy. They found him weeping. "There really was a wolf here! The flock has scattered! I cried out, "Wolf!" Why didn't you come?"

An old man tried to comfort the boy as they walked back to the village.

"We'll help you look for the lost sheep in the morning," he said, putting his arm around the youth, "Nobody believes a liar...even when he is telling the truth!" (43)

Much better than that the leader continually reminds everyone of the end goal required of the strategic plan, as well as deciding whether to employ a strategy that releases Potential Energy, (for example, by moving individuals and teams into a high priority project, or by using a strategy based on Elastic Energy, or giving a motivated team a challenge where the resources and capabilities don't quite match).

The leader should continually 'check in' with their managers to gain their feedback on the effectiveness of *Set the Velocity*, paying particular attention to any major energy blockages. Those need to swiftly be removed by a range of tactics which managers will put into practice. This could involve splitting or moving individuals and teams around the workplace, taking specific interventions to help improve behaviour, skills and capabilities needed, adapting or closing down programmes.

In this context, *Praise and Commemorate* and *Carry the Can* have an additional and important function. They help the leader pace energy in the workplace. Taking time out to learn from mistakes or celebrate successes are one way the leader can ensure the workplace won't burnout energetically as Rest energy takes place in these moments of reflection.

8 - Observe the Flow

The leader shouldn't be so busy in their own work that they stop noticing the rate of energy in the workplace. In effect, they need to be aware and stay ahead of the pace. They do this by 'Observe the Flow'.

It may seem that a leader behind a desk watching and waiting and seeming to do nothing is an awful waste of a big salary. Not so!

Think back to *The Heart of the Matter*. The Leader's use of Energy Intelligence after she has given the green light for the heart transplant process to begin is an observational role. This can be a lonely place because the connection to the action is detached, yet she is joined to the result.

As Observer, the leader plays a crucial role in witnessing the workplace in energy flow. Despite the temptation to get involved and to find out what's going on, she remains present, open to the possibilities of what might occur. If she were 'in the flow' doing the work, she wouldn't be able to see what was unfolding.

Fig 10. Superfocus

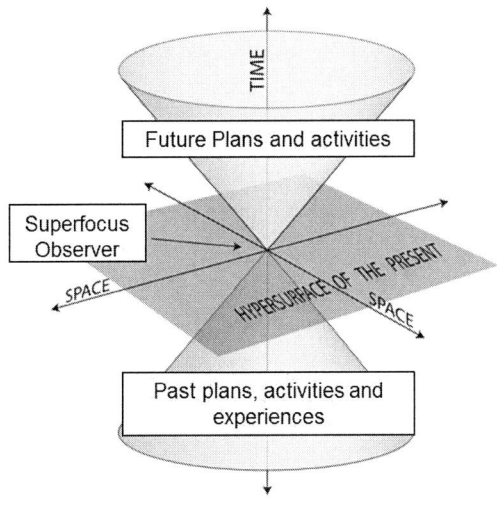

The leader is in a state of 'Superfocus' of concentrated observation. This can only happen if she isn't distracted i.e. she has made the *Decide and Stick* decision and *Leave Well Alone*. Now, she can focus completely on the present, recording and noting what is taking place without applying thoughts or feelings to the process. It is as if she stands apart from the action and in that moment is removed from it as if she is watching what happens from a different vantage point, just like a camera documenting what takes place. Her own ego with its emotions, bias and interest is kept in check and she has no expectations, pre-conditions or premonitions about what has or might happen. Everything is in motion and *is what it is*.

In the book Presence, Peter Senge describes the camera or 'Superfocus' state as *Presencing*: "You observe and observe and let this experience well up into something appropriate. In a sense, there's no decision-making. What you do just becomes obvious. You can't rush it. Much of it depends on where you're coming from and what you do as a person. All you can do is position yourself according to your unfolding vision of what is coming. A totally different set of rules applies. You need to 'feel out' what you do." (44)

The Leader is letting things happen without intervention and as patterns emerge and work (or not) she is able to intervene if appropriate, at the right time, to make strategic decisions to improve and shape the future. She spots the connections between what is past and what is yet to come.

In *The Heart of the Matter*, her intervention comes at the end of the process in the form of a celebration. In an alternative scenario, if things hadn't worked out, she may change the pattern by revising *Decide and Stick* through taking a different decision, changing members of the team or even reviewing the vision of the service to see if it's fit for purpose to deliver heart transplants. If a new model is operated, it will have to be trailed and tested until it works as well as the previous set-up before it went wrong.

In the Theory of Relativity $E=MC^2$, the Observer acts as a reference frame, describing what happens in time and space in an independent manner. They are inert, measuring a set of objects or events, the witness to what is going on and what takes place becomes observer dependant. For what is witnessed from the outside looking in is different to what is experienced on the inside. With Energy Intelligence, the Observer has a similar role.

"Imagine a police officer chasing after a speeding motorist. If he drives fast enough, the officer knows that he can catch the motorist. Anyone who has ever gotten a ticket for speeding knows that. But if we now replace the speeding motorist with a light beam, and an observer witnesses the whole thing, then the observer concludes that the officer is speeding just behind the light beam, travelling almost as fast as light. We are confident that the officer knows he is travelling neck and neck with the light beam.

But later, when we interview him, we hear a strange tale. He claims that instead of riding alongside the light beam as we just witnessed, it sped away from him, leaving him in the dust. He says that no matter how much he gunned his engines, the light beam sped away at precisely the same velocity. In fact, he swears that he could not even make a dent in catching up to the light beam. No matter how fast he travelled, the light beam travelled away from him at the speed of light, as if he were stationary instead of speeding in a police car.

But when you insist that you saw the police officer speeding neck and neck with the light beam, within a hairsbreadth of catching up to it, he says you are crazy; he never even got close. To Einstein, this was the central, nagging mystery: *How was it possible for two people to see the same event in such totally different ways?* If the speed of light was really a constant of nature, then how could a witness claim that the officer was neck and neck with the light beam, yet the officer swears that he never even got close?

Although we usually think of lengths and times as absolute, they turned out to be observer-dependent. Ordinarily, we think of velocities as relative, but one of them turns out to be absolute: the speed of light." (45)

In this context, the Leader is like an experimenter looking at events taking place away from herself but seeing the coincidences between these events and the local attributes of them. She is the constant in the picture.

Fortunately, most Leaders won't have to observe events unfolding at the speed of light! But what they will witness are tiny relativistic effects at the speeds encountered in the workplace and unless someone concentrates on looking for them, they will pass unnoticed. These tiny events will build over time to form a new energetic paradigm and by the time the change is noticed, it may be too late to take remedial action to break workplace habits, processes, rituals and routines.

Generally, we are poor observers. Our attention span is short and our minds wander. Leaders need to hone their observation skills and the results will come, but not quickly. There are several ways one can develop observational skills. They include practising mindfulness, being still, meditation, yoga, prayer, tai chi and mindful walking.

9 - Shoot the Moon

"Alice laughed: "There's no use trying," she said; "one can't believe impossible things."

"I daresay you haven't had much practice," said the Queen. "When I was younger, I always did it for half an hour a day. Why, sometimes I've believed as many as six impossible things before breakfast." (46)

Most innovation has come from people refusing to accept the status quo. They believed flying in the air or travelling across the sea could be possible and the way of doing it hadn't been found. They set about the task of realising this and through the ages, artists and scientists have proved the impossible to be possible.

If the workplace is to shift its way of thinking and acting, it needs to get out of working to established norms and consider radical, new ways of looking at what they do.

The leader plays a role hereto 'Shoot the Moon' by asking the impossible. This can be done by posing a series of what I call 'impossible questions' for the workplace to answer and *to keep on asking them as the project unfolds until they become viable.*

In her book *Glow*, Dr Lynda Gratton introduces the concept of 'igniting questions'. She gives the example of Ratan Tata, the Chairman of the Tata Group. He asked why a car couldn't be built for £100,000 rupees (at current exchange rates, less than £2,000) affordable to families as well as safe, fuel-efficient and low on emissions.

"As one of the engineers told me: *It seemed like an absolutely impossible question. No one could believe we could do it. There was a lot of cynicism-people thought we would just make motorcycles joined at the hip or a supercharged auto rickshaw. But we were determined to do it. It meant going back to basics, re-engineering many of the parts, working closely with our component suppliers such as Bosch, and fundamentally questioning the way we do everything.*" (47)

The car was launched to great acclaim in 2009 and billed as 'the world's cheapest' car. But the igniting question posed proved to be unworkable. Since *Glow* was written, the Nano car has failed miserably on the safety front, falling short on global crash test standards and sales have recently been sluggish.

By 2014, Tata realised that billing the car as 'the world's cheapest' car was a mistake. "That moniker has not served it well, making the car sound flimsy and unreliable instead of no-frills and accessible.....

In the meantime, Tata is chiselling the Nano's image and nudging the price up with every change. January saw the launch of the revamped, slightly dearer Nano Twist. New features like power-steering and a digital music system should thrill the kids, but I imagine they'd be more pleased with the intervention of an airbag in the event of a high-speed collision. Just an idea." (48)

So, the leader needs to do more than ask *an* igniting question. They need to observe as the process of development unfolds and *keep on* asking impossible questions and encourage their managers to do the same. In the case of the Nano car, once the design and cost came in on budget, further questions like 'is being 'cheap' a good branding proposition?' and 'do poor people have lower expectations of safety?' could have had impact. Perhaps asking a question like 'what have we stopped doing'? or using my 'What Why' process throughout the project could have had profound consequences for the Nano car!

So could Dr. Edward de Bono's technique Provocative Operations which is also known as 'PO'(49). In this process, a 'statement' (see below) is generated that might not make sense but can be used to create movement to a new idea. In a sense, the mind is unsettled through the use of five formal methods for generating provocations. These are *escape, reversal, distortion, exaggeration* and *wishful thinking* and have often led to innovation.

For example:

Escape - (Pick something taken for granted and drop it.)

Statement: Restaurants have seats.
Statement: Restaurants have no seats.
Statement: Charge for a seat.

"Walk past many cafes during the daytime and you'll see people sitting inside, nursing a coffee as they work away at their laptops. If you're spending all day buying one expensive coffee after another, though, the costs can really add up.

But for those who work outside of the traditional office environment, there is a potential new alternative - pay-per-minute cafes.

Ziferblat is a concept that has already proved popular in Russia - and now the chain has opened its first cafe in London's Old Street.

The founders say, "everything is free, except the time you spend there". Customers pay 3p per minute - or £1.80 an hour - for unlimited food, coffee and access to Wi-Fi. You can even bring your own food or drink." (50)

The key thing here is that leader and workplace managers should be trained in lateral thinking techniques to pose questions from statements like the above e.g. we have a chain of coffee shops. Should we have seating? They should consider all the positives and negatives posed through the 'What Why' process before making any changes and any major new process should be observed by the leader as described in *Observe the Flow*.

So, the leader's role is to ask the 'big' fundamental questions. Anita Roddick, founder of the Body Shop asked herself what seemed to be at the time, two impossible questions that challenged the norms of the day. "It wasn't only economic necessity that inspired the birth of The Body Shop. Her early travels gave her a wealth of experience. She had spent time in farming and fishing communities with pre-industrial peoples, and was exposed to body rituals of women from all over the world. Also the frugality that her mother exercised during the war years made her question retail conventions. *Why waste a container when you can refill it? And why buy more of something than you can use?* She behaved as her mother had in World War II. The Body Shop reused everything, refilled everything and recycled all they could. The foundation of The Body Shop's environmental activism was born out of these ideas. (51) (Italics mine.)

Google has a research facility in the USA called 'Google X'. In its Moonshot Factory, inventors and engineers work up ideas and possibilities that may bring about huge, transformational change. The 'Captain of Moonshots' is Astro Teller, the grandson of theoretical physicist Edward Teller.

Perhaps he is the most radical example of an Energy Intelligent leader practicing *Shoot the Moon*. He encourages colleagues to identify a problem by posing a series of questions. "As an example, he cites the problem of a million people dying on the roads each year. The science fiction solution it came up with was driverless cars that don't crash. Google has now clocked up hundreds of thousands of miles of testing that suggests this technology will work and could transform our world." (52)

The questions posed are designed to solve problems. Making money is not the core issue. Income will come into the company he says in an 'elegant way' if the problem gets solved!

Everything Google X does is linked to the following three aspirations.

1. It has to potentially solve a really big problem for the world - it has to help millions or billions of people
2. It has to be radical, science-fiction sounding technology (e.g. cars that drive themselves)
3. It has to show some progress that gives a glimmer of hope that the sci-fi-sounding solution might actually be possible.

"Things like search or translate, things like maps, have been in the public domain free to the users but often without advertising or any form of compensation - sometimes for many years - when Google didn't make money on it or even have a plan to make money on it and Google was just 'Let's make value for the users. We'll figure out how to make money later'." (52)

10 - Work with Radiance

When the workplace is consistently delivering successful outcomes and is showing signs of *Radiant Energy*, the impact of this on the external environment can be immense.

Radiant energy produced in the workplace will positively affect the external environment in unpredictable, non-standardised ways. In a sense, the changes will happen beyond the conscious senses of the organisation. Over time, some of the Radiant energy will re-enter the workplace in ways that couldn't have been predicted.

Fig 11. Radiant Energy at Work

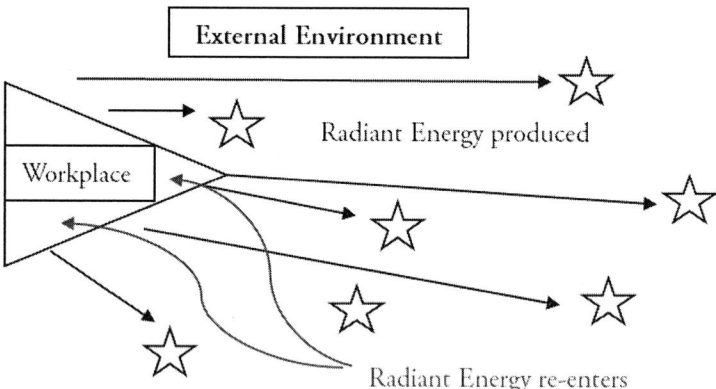

The leader needs to understand this fundamental principle of Radiant energy and its synchronous effects. They must expect to be pleasantly surprised about the fact that Radiant energy supplies unexpected benefits and work with them when they come and wherever they come from! Examples of how Radiant energy may re-enter the workplace include staff and customers who have had a good experience telling others who tell other people and just as the workplace decides to expand its operations in another sector, someone from that sector gets in touch asking to do business with them. Non ENQ workplaces will say things like 'they are lucky' or 'what a coincidence'. Energy Intelligent people will realise that this is Radiant energy in operation.

In my own experience, I have received the benefits of Radiant Energy to the point where I expect something to happen but I don't know how or what. But I know it will be positive and beneficial. I once coached a delightful woman who was considering whether she should take her family to another country and begin to develop a dream she'd had to build a hotel in a third world country. After much thought and deliberation, she made the decision and it has proven to be very successful. Several months later, when I was thinking about how I could meet globally influential people I could share my Energy Intelligence ideas with, I was contacted by a friend of the woman I'd helped. She too asked for a coaching session to make a big life choice and in doing so, recommended me to her 'boss' who is an extremely well-connected entrepreneur. I am now working as a consultant in her company which gives me opportunities to travel and to meet and share my ideas with people from different cultural backgrounds to mine.

11 - Ask Bob

In one of my jobs in local government, there was an amazing man called Bob. Bob had started working for the council when he was sixteen. Over the course of his career, he changed jobs several times and ended up running the Civic Centre. If anyone wanted to know something about anything, the answer would always be "Ask Bob." He could remember facts about things long forgotten. He could put his hands on paperwork that explained decisions made. He could tell you why doing something that you thought was new and innovative had been tried before (at least twice) and which bits had succeeded and failed and why. In truth, Bob was a fountain of knowledge and a very valuable resource. He understood and could extract what I call 'the workplace DNA'. He retired aged sixty. As his leaving date became due, I was puzzled that nobody had asked him to record his thoughts or to leave a system that others could use. Nor had he been asked to train anyone up to take this place.

When he left, a lot of people scratched their heads trying to remember or find things that Bob could have sorted in moments. A lot of time and energy was wasted.

The law of Conservation of Energy states that the (total) energy of a system can increase or decrease only by transferring it in or out of the system. In the case of Bob, when he transferred out of the workplace on his retirement, a hell of a lot of energy stored in his memories and experience left with him!

The collective memory of the workplace needs safeguarding lest it be forgotten so that avoidable mistakes aren't made that de-energise everyone.

The leader should recognise the importance of keeping a *learning library* of all the decisions made, lessons learned and the *quirkiness* of it all. What I mean by this is that it's not just about storing information in a database. The library needs to be brought together by a conservator who can reflect the idiosyncratic nature of the workplace. The conservator has to be a person trained in conservation, collation and reference skills and ideally can pull things together and interpret them with a humorous, even satirical eye. This will make accessing any information far more interesting, motivational and fun!

Who better to take on the task of collating workplace learning and turning it into an accessible library than a qualified librarian?

When I began my career, most local authorities had a 'Bob', a Corporate Librarian' doing the above.

Workplaces are swamped with information. It's readily accessible at the click of a search engine. But it's *what we do with it* that counts. What many people don't realise in the internet age is that the retrieval of information and *making sense of it* is a skill that is a science and then arguably over time becomes an art that most people don't possess. Librarians go to library school to do degrees in their subject.

Sadly, the position of Corporate Librarian went early on in cost-cutting exercises, to be replaced by fragmented memories housed on individual data bases and word documents.

The Energy Intelligent Leader has the role of Curator of the Workplace DNA. It is their ultimate responsibility to be the keeper of it until they hand the baton onto a new leader at some point in the future. The Corporate Librarian works to them, conserving the knowledge of what's gone before, researching and supplying information on potential energy in staff and giving their views on the likely probability of something working based on past plans, activities and experiences.

This will aid the leader and managers in making future decisions.

12 - Be a Time Lord

In the BBC science fiction television series Doctor Who, Time Lords (the Doctor is a member) are an ancient extra-terrestrial civilisation of humanoid species. Here are some of the characteristics of a Time Lord:

- They have *a non-linear perception of time* that allows them to see everything in the past, present or future.
- *They are custodians with a duty of care for others,* to prevent time from being subverted or abused by others.
- *They operate a non-interference and neutrality policy.*
- *They can manipulate timelines* and events as long as they don't cross back into their own timeline.
- *They are a non-violent race.*
- *They live a long time* and can absorb radiation and x-rays and cope with extreme heat and cold compared to humans.
- *They can communicate by telepathy and link their minds to others,* sharing information and enhancing their powers.
- *They can regenerate their bodies* when mortally wounded into a new form and personality. (53)

In a sense, a leader who practices *'Set the Direction', Ask Bob', 'Set the Velocity'* and *'Shoot the Moon'* will develop a **non-linear time perspective**. Very few workplaces understand what the landscape they want to operate in the future will look like, yet they can do this by engaging The Sensory Landscape process I describe on page 83. *Ask Bob* brings information from the past that can be used to inform decision-making and *Set the Velocity* keeps an energetic pace flowing in the present moving towards the future through questions asked in *Shoot the Moon*.

All of these ways of doing and being help the leader understand the flow of time better but the key thing is *Observe the flow*. In practicing this, the leader is taken 'out of the present time flow' that the team is working in and from their observational vantage point, is able to see connections between the past and future, present and past and future and past. As the connections become clear, the leader can then *act* but until that point, they operate **a non-interference and neutrality policy.** Once they step out of Observing the Flow, they are **manipulating timelines and events** by changing the prioritisation and timing of projects or altering the staffing and resourcing of them. This happens **as long as they don't cross back into their own timeline** for if they do, they will be back in Observing the Flow which is a state of inaction.

Align the Values and *Carry the Can* provides an agreed set of behaviours that all people in the workplace comply with. Like the Time Lord, the leader has a **duty of care for others** and lives, uses and supports the values as a way of life. An Energy Intelligent organisation practices **non-violence** in all its forms e.g. a lack of hostility, fierceness, aggression through the example set by their leader.

I'm not sure we are there yet in relation to being able to **communicate by telepathy and link their minds to others, sharing information and enhancing their powers.** But Energy Intelligent workplaces have a greater degree of mutual understanding because so many things are shared for example values, asking impossible questions, celebrating. People become more perceptive and thoughtful towards each other in this environment and the desire to work together co-operatively means information is shared not held. This gives deeper insight and understanding and minds are linked in a shared purpose. When they reach a state of energy synchronicity, similar ideas abound as if communicated by a telepathic link?

Energy Intelligent leaders have the tools I've described in this book to bring their workplaces back from the brink of being toxic. The ability to turnaround radioactive workplaces and re-energise them means their careers last longer than most at the top. In effect, **they live a long time and can absorb radiation and x-rays!**

Finally, when it's time to move on or retire, they know their custodial role is over. They pass on the baton to a new leader who is well aware of working in an Energy Intelligent workplace. **They can regenerate their bodies when mortally wounded into a new form and personality.** (This may be in the persona of glorious retirement on a golf course, doing charitable works or travel, but whatever it is, they've deserved it!)

---

13   Lose Your Ego

Energy Intelligent leaders will have followers. If their workplace is displaying high Energy Intelligence, it will in part, be due to the leader's ability to motivate and inspire colleagues to perform at their best. So, they will be authentic and charming and kind to people whether they are speaking to large audiences, small groups or individuals and will have an open, friendly disposition.

Energy Intelligent leaders don't have to be charismatic. Far from it! Often, leaders with this magnetism start to believe in their own myth and want to be adored. They place themselves 'out front' and success becomes *all about them* as they bathe in reflective glory. In their quest for 'ego massage', they can lose sight of The Baker's Dozen and their core function; to manage the motivation of staff and energy flow of the workplace.

The ENQ leader knows when to lead from the front and when to take a back seat to let others do what they can't do. In *The Heart of the Matter*, if I hadn't told you the leader was the woman sitting behind the desk, you may not have realised? In many ways, in that moment, she seemed to lack personality and appeal, to be *insignifi-*

cant. She left her ego under her desk and let others take central stage to play their part. She is the director and producer, not the lead actor.

Some of the most successful leaders in history have displayed similar qualities. In the UK, it can be argued that Prime Ministers like Clement Atlee and John Major pushed through policies that unified and supported people from different political persuasions and backgrounds. Yet, they couldn't be described as charismatic or ego-driven.

Charismatic leaders like Margaret Thatcher and Tony Blair drew political and social 'lines in the sand' that separated people. It could be argued that when successful policies were attributed to them, their ego grew and this sustained a further energetic response. Often, when the ego is involved and the leader is charismatic, they need more success to fuel themselves and they don't practice Rest energy.

Their workplace energy overheats, they drop to the Stress Energy Tensor (see fig 4 on page 36). They stop practising The Baker's Dozen, especially *Observing* and *Ask Bob*. As they move swiftly down into the unhealthy energy zone, they can even forget the mission, vision and values that have brought them to power. Then, they lose sight of *Decide and Stick* and *Leave Well Alone* and begin deciding what's best for everyone when the evidence of information and feelings of the majority of people and the timing of the decision don't bear this out. Then, Radioactive energy is produced and the leader becomes toxic. The Council Tax and the Iraq War are examples of policies created by leaders who can't *Leave Their Ego*. The party vote, the ballot box, public enquiries and history have judged them.

....

Now that you have read Chapter seven, it is time to review your skills and activities as an Energy Intelligent Leader and to review your own practice of The Baker's Dozen.

In doing so you might ask 'how Energy Intelligent am I as a leader?' or perhaps you are contemplating a leadership role and wish to consider your preparation for the role and responsibilities.

Try the questions below answering simple Yes or No.

1. Have you reviewed your organisational mission statement in the last year?
2. Do you engage your top team in discussions of your vision for the organisation?
3. Are your personal values in keeping with those of your organisation?
4. Are your organisational values shared by employees and evident in activities?
5. Do you communicate clearly about your major decisions?
6. Is there clear evidence of the successful implementation of strategic priorities?
7. Are you able to trust your managers and teams to deliver without your intervention?
8. Do you spend at least a fifth of your time 'walking the floor'?
9. Do you recognise, praise and thank your staff for their achievements and commitment?
10. Can you identify weaknesses or faults within your organisation?
11. Do you acknowledge weaknesses and state clearly the remedial action to be taken?
12. Are strategic priorities regularly reviewed with your top team?
13. Do your senior managers inform you of progress blocks and adjust action accordingly?

14. Is there time in your week for regular observation of work and energy flow?
15. Do you ask fundamental /challenging/'impossible' questions related to the work your organisation undertakes?
16. Are your senior managers encouraged to ask fundamental /challenging/'impossible' questions of their teams?
17. Do your attitudes convey an expectation of success?
18. Are you positive about success, recognising it will naturally flow within your organisation?
19. Do you ensure major decisions and successes are recorded?
20. Is a learning library of decisions, outcomes and lessons available for staff to consult?
21. Are you able to step outside current events and see links between past and future?
22. Do you seek to set an example of non-violence, avoiding hostility and aggression?
23. Are you willing to take a back seat in the limelight and give credit to others who deserve it?
24. Do you practice kindness and humility as a leader?

So how did you get on? It is natural that you may find yourself feeling resistant in some areas or want to answer 'No', or 'sometimes', 'occasionally', 'if...' for some questions. This suggests that more consideration should be given to these areas.

For each questions that you were unable to answer 'yes' to, it is important to consider what support and action you might take. Writing a personal log about issues that arise is likely to be helpful. Discussing issues with selected and trustworthy confidantes or possibly a coach or mentor might also be of benefit especially if they are willing and able to give you honest, supportive and constructive feedback. Identifying personal goals and a timeframe for action is important so that you can take steps to change, so that you are able to increase your Energy Intelligence as a leader and in so doing enhance the effectiveness of your organisation.

Chapter summary

In this chapter we have considered The Baker's Dozen features necessary for the Energy Intelligent leader. A set of twenty four questions have been included at the end of the chapter so that you are able to reflect on your own style, skills and approaches, and to think about how this translates into action for you as a leader and the effects that has on the organisation. This will help you to identify areas in which you are already practicing Energy Intelligence effectively, in addition to highlighting areas in which you might be more effective.

In the next chapter, we will consider the characteristics of the Energy Intelligent manager.

CHAPTER 8

Energy Intelligent Managers

Chapter overview

In this chapter, managers have the fundamental role as a 'Connector'. This role is about paying close attention to the energy flow and its regulation in the workplace. This involves uniting colleagues for activity and task completion, identifying problems and solutions, making links and disconnections as required.

In order to be effective, six characteristics of Energy Intelligent Managers, are referred to as "Six of the Best". These are: Crafter, Sensor, Reporter, Animator, Streamer and Enquirer. As with the previous chapter, a set of questions is included for you to think about your effectiveness as a manager, or to review your preparation for undertaking managerial responsibilities in a future role. Actions are suggested to take which will strengthen your skills and abilities.

If the role of leading the workplace involves practicing 'The Baker's Dozen', leaders should be removed from day to day operations, working remotely as Energy Intelligent Leaders. In the Energy Intelligent workplace, managers are in effect left to 'get on with it'!

Henry Minzberg is his book 'Managing' states: "It has become popular to talk about us being over managed and under led. I believe *we are now over led and under managed.*"(54) I agree with Mintzberg for Energy Intelligence places management at *the centre of the action* giving the Energy Intelligent Manager a set of objectives crucial to the performance of the workplace.

By 'managers', I mean anyone who has the role and responsibility for a group of people and delivery of projects, programmes, services and associated activities. Their job title may include the words manager, head of, supervisor, superintendent, team leader, group leader, coordinator and so on.

In the Energy Intelligent workplace, the *fundamental purpose of the manager is the role of Connector,* giving managers the freedom to unite and bond the workplace and continue to fix it in a way that they've never had before.

If I want power in the form of electricity to go into my PC or my television, I'll need an interface to join my machines to the electricity supply. Connectors consist of plugs (male ended) and jacks (female ended) and there are hundreds of different types of electrical connectors just as there are male and female managers!

I use the right kind of connector and attach it to the back of my television. The other end plugs into the electric socket. The TV has power and I can watch my favourite programmes.

Six of the Best

The 'right kind of connector' in Energy Intelligent workplaces is the manager who delivers six areas of responsibility:

- To join people together to complete a task
- To fix problems and find solutions
- To bond colleagues through positive behaviours
- To unite people by motivating them
- To disconnect people who are not committed to the workplace

- To link people through effective communication

They do this through six distinct characteristics I call 'Six of the Best'.

---

1 - Crafter

As a consultant, I often get called in to support managers and teams who aren't working well together. Often, what it boils down to is people who are doing work they hate, find boring or simply have too much of it to cope. They lose energy and come off the pace. Colleagues get irritated and think 'Fred is 'swinging the lead' again. Who does he think he is? Why should I work hard if he's taking it easy?' or they get stressed and then their behaviour degenerates and they provoke others e.g. by being snappy, argumentative and rude.

Here's the thing. I don't like routine. I like my day to be changeable, even unpredictable. I positively enjoy a change. For me it's as good as a rest as I'm stimulated and my creative juices flow. Other people would find that scary if not stressful. They like to know what they are going to do that day. They have a routine and are much happier when they can get into the rhythm of it. Neither position is right or wrong. We need people who enjoy and are good at maintaining processes and systems just as we need people who will generate new ideas to create new ways of doing things.

Most people exist on a spectrum across the extremes I've described, with a lot of work they'd expect to do with a few surprises occasionally thrown into the mix. It's what each of us *prefers* that counts. Wouldn't it be great to work in a place where you can do what you prefer? Sounds like an impossible task but it isn't really.

When I ask people to share what they love and hate doing in their work, I often find there are others in the team who love to do things others hate and vice versa. The solution then is to give people the work they love and see whether everyone has enough to do. It usually works out well as long as people are prepared to give things up that they hate to take on what they like!

Energy Intelligent Managers make it their business to find out as much as they can about the people they co-ordinate. This includes knowing all the things they've done before they joined the workplace so that the Potential Energy of all of the skills, knowledge and experience of their team is understood.

They have ongoing conversations on an individual and group basis to check that people's expertise is being used fully and that people are motivated and happy.

They craft meaningful work based on what they know and the conversations they are having, playing to the strengths and talents of individuals. If I'm naturally more creative, why not give me a problem to solve or a new project to realise? Perhaps the manager as *Crafter* can put people with creative ideas into a small research and development team who meet up occasionally to come up with new ideas? If I enjoy routine and repetitive tasks, why give that to someone who hates detail and will get bored easily and make mistakes? Far better to hand out work like this to someone who enjoys getting things right and teams of people with these attributes could be asked to work together to do quality assurance projects!

Managers should construct their teams carefully to make sure they have the right blend of attributes to make work a pleasure and a success for all concerned.

I mentioned previously, there is in any workplace, a 'rump' of people who have hit a wall in their career where they know they are unlikely to progress further (and nor in many cases do they want to). Whilst they do a reasonable job, they are what I call 'cruising in neutral'! It is to this group the manager needs to turn their attention as the *Rest energy* levels are higher than elsewhere. The manager has to set specific projects and targets over time and consistently check that work is progressing. After every effort has been made to craft meaningful work for 'Fred' because he is coasting along and not motivated like his colleagues (or indeed supportive of them), the manager's role is to 'disconnect' Fred. This may involve giving him training, personal development, asking his colleagues to support and challenge him, or moving him to another team. Ultimately, it is Fred's responsibility to develop himself. All you as his manager can do is help him to do this.

If none of these interventions work and Fred's energy and motivation is still low, his services may be no longer required in an Energy Intelligent workplace. It may be a harsh form of treatment, but if everyone knows this is a possibility from the onset because it forms part of the Commitment Contract.

2 - Sensor

The manager will have been involved in the Sensory Landscape process and will have a clear picture of the end result three or five years into the future (up the stairs) of where the workplace wants to be and how it will be behaving and performing energetically. As I described on page 83, the Sensory Landscape process also works backwards in time (down the stairs), highlighting all the actions that need to take place and the people who are needed to complete them to the present time period.

The manager's role is to 'read' the sensory landscape as it emerges step by step. They will know from the detailed action planning that at a specific point in time on the staircase, specific actions should have been completed engaging explicit behaviours and using a defined amount of energy. They have to 'sense' where things are at by listening, feeling, noticing and even smelling out what's going on. If they don't feel their team is performing to the desired levels, they first need to check in with their colleagues, to discuss what's happening and try to resolve any issues that arise.

Another important function of *Sensor* is that of reminding people who are working hard in the present, what they are aiming towards in the future. This helps to motivate and bond people towards the agreed common goal and can act as a positive 'check in' that their behaviours and actions are aligned to the sensory landscape outcome.

The manager should also be informing the workplace leader of any changes to the sensory landscape, what they have done about it to bring things back on track and/or if that's not possible, to discuss with the leader what impact this will have on the workplace strategy.

In my very first senior manager role, when I asked my CEO what he expected of me, he replied: 'No surprises.' He meant that if anything was amiss, he would like to be informed as it was happening, not when it was too late to do anything about it!

3 - Reporter

Managers are a vital conduit in passing information along communication channels (especially up to workplace leaders and down to their teams). The role of *Reporter* is to know what's going on and to pass on this information in an even-handed, open-minded way. As a

Reporter, they provide an account of their team's work and behaviour, providing the leader with a commentary on *how things are*. They become an 'investigative' reporter when they sense something is wrong, nosing out the issues and proposing remedial action. This should be in the form of a regular statement preferably given orally, but failing that, in a report.

In the same way, managers should inform their teams of any changes within the workplace that may affect them. Ideally, managers should see their leader on a regular basis to get an account from them as well as receiving a weekly briefing note direct from the leader.

Managers link people together and they should be mindful of passing on all messages in an unbiased, objective manner, for they are the nerve of operations, the communications centre of their teams. As soon as they present information or communicate it with a slant or bias, they become 'political players', looking out for their own advancement and for those they favour. Instead of uniting people, they split or disconnect them. **There are no political players in an Energy Intelligent organisation.** Unscrupulous, sly or cunning behaviour should look so out of place and tawdry, the fact that others find it distasteful and don't play the game should be enough of a signal to the 'player' that the game is over. In the rare case that politics is played on, they should be challenged by the team and the leader to desist and ultimately, they may have to leave the workplace on the basis that 'this isn't something we do around here'!

The manager as *Reporter* involves disseminating information and cross-pollinating it between people and groups. They do this well and without bias and they earn the trust and respect of their teams to be their spokesperson.

The *Reporter* role can also add great value to the workplace Learning Library by providing copy for the workplace 'Testimony Book' which is collated by the Corporate Librarian. This involves giving information, personal insights and thoughts on managerial interventions that did or didn't work to be compiled into a handbook of management for the workplace.

The Testimony Book provides living evidence and demonstration of Energy Intelligent management in the workplace. It can be accessed by anyone to use and even used as the basis for action learning for managers so that they can sit back alone or in groups to reflect on their own practice and that of other managers.

As managing can at times seem to be very reactive, this is the one opportunity a manager has to step out of the action, reflect and alter their modus operandi. In creative thinking and problem-solving processes, there always has to be a time for reflection to allow the problem or challenge to be understood. During one of the early phases in the creative thinking process (called the 'incubation phase'), spending time thinking about possible alternative ways of tackling an issue can provide great insight, even illumination. Mimicking other manager's methods that have been proven to work, can provide a fast-track route to success rather than testing out, failing and having to try something else. They learn 'on the job' using the experiences of other colleagues as their guide. The added benefit is when 'Bob' has left the workplace and it's too late to *Ask Bob* anything, his experience and thinking will be found in the Testimony Book.

---

4 - Animator

Equally important is the manager's ability to bring out the best in people and motivate them through developing and testing personal relationships with individuals they supervise. They should do this with an informal style and system of communication, meeting face-to-face ideally where their teams are located. As the manager understands their team's abilities and their potential, a key role of *Animator* is to place the right people together to maximise individual and collective creativity to complete a task. As *Animator*, the manager should give people the freedom to do their work as they have been professionally trained to do. In a sense, they are stirring a pot of professionals!

Mistakes made, even failure, should be treated as a learning experience and the manager should animate people to consider what has been learned in the process, so that individuals and teams don't lose their energy and motivation. "Success consists of going from failure to failure without losing enthusiasm," said Winston Churchill. (55) If not handled in this way, the sense of failure will eat away at people's motivation and their desire to take calculated risks. They play safe, only doing what they know has worked in the past and cruise along in neutral in their comfort zone. They risk losing the ability to surpass what they believed to be possible; to make the impossible possible!

Mistakes are often made for a reason and understanding what they are and why this has happened can often provide insights and important solutions. The key thing is that the same mistakes should not be repeated and any setback if used as a key learning experience without apportioning blame, will keep the team's focus on wanting success in the present moving into the future, not wasting energy in the past and the errors made.

Mihaly Csíkszentmihályi Flow Diagram (56) can be gainfully used by Animators to assess their team's motivational and energetic state. By employing techniques described in the *Enquirer* characteristic, managers can find out where individuals are positioned.

The flow state highlighted is the equivalent of an energy state above the Stress Energy Tensor (see p36), where E = MCC (where energy and motivation and commitment are in balance and equal to each other.) If managers ask their staff how they are and they reply that they are worried or bored, it's clear that the challenge they have been set may be too difficult (e.g. they don't have enough time or resources to complete it), or the skills they have are being under-used or are too repetitive so they are not challenged. They are out of flow and if that continues, they will drop down the Energy Spectrum.

Fig 12. Flow diagram

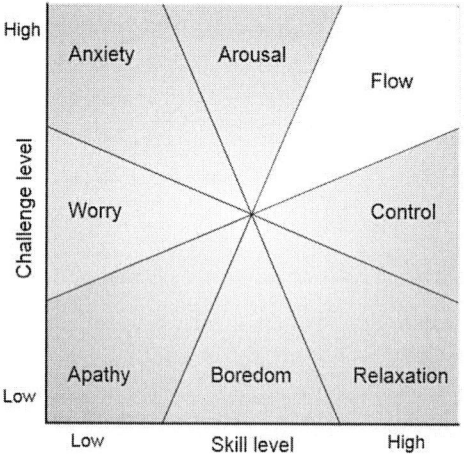

Ideally, the manager's role as *Animator* is to juggle the skills of the people they have to suit the challenges they face. It's a constant process of refinement where managers test, discuss and apply.

Giving people the freedom to control their work and to be excited by the challenge of it will mean Energy Intelligence over time.

The *Animator* manager does everything in their power to minimise the thresholds of low challenge and skill usage in their teams.

5   Streamer

Whilst the leader *Sets the Pace* of the energy in the workplace, the manager *maintains its current*. I call this characteristic of Energy Intelligent management the *Streamer*. You may have heard of the term 'live streaming' which refers to content delivered over the internet. In the early days of live streaming, films and music ran slow or froze because there wasn't enough power in a computer or network bandwidth capacity.

The manager as *Streamer* ensures that at any given time, there is enough power directed towards the project (in the form of the type of energy employed). If more power is needed to shift things, Potential energy may be employed or Elastic energy. If too much power is being used and teams are burning out of ideas, motivation or practical application, then Rest energy may be applied. Sometimes, bringing in other teams or individuals to solve a problem, can increase bandwidth capacity.

When I was asked to manage the re-design of a museum, I put together small teams of people with a good mix of skills, knowledge, experience and energetic pace in their professional areas and set them the task of delivering a museum that would be the 'best in the southwest'. We employed the Sensory Landscape process so we all had a clear picture of how we wanted the museum to be operating two years hence.

One team was looking at a new local history service where people could come and find out about the history of the town and its people. Another assessed the museum collections and how they could be displayed and accessed to maximum effect. Another considered how the building could be adapted to make it a landmark space in the town.

The local history team did a decent job on how visitors could use the facilities to research their family history, or an aspect of industrial heritage. The museums team worked well on how to alter the space in the museum differently to fit in small (pottery collections) and large (boats and vehicles) exhibitions. The building team worked with in-house architects, coming up with possible building alterations and designs.

The enthusiasm from all people involved was high, but energy levels and focus differed and started to affect the overall shape of the scheme. I sensed that the building team became less energetic over time. They seemed constrained by the footprint of the existing museum which was located in a conservation area and some of the problems they encountered (the building was listed and areas of it were inaccessible) made their enthusiasm flag. Money which was to be spent on design was being moved towards dealing with the mechanical and engineering issues they found.

The local history team were plodding along and getting very involved in the detail. Rather than thinking about the sensory landscape of the new service and imagining how it could be as a customer experience, they were working on how to catalogue photographs and documents and then to find a computer system that could cope with everything.

The museums team began to run into difficulties because the building team lost energy and they couldn't be sure the space they needed would be provided.

So, I considered the energetic workings of the teams and decided it was critical to 'increase the bandwidth' of the buildings team by bringing in an internationally famous architect who had personal links to the town to provide a fresh perspective. I invited him to join the team and ask 'impossible questions' even when it appeared that its listed building status wouldn't allow it e.g. 'Can we get rid of this part of the building?' These questions seemed to unblock the teams' energy flow and in answering him, they realised the entrance to the building could be removed, as it was a later extension with no architectural merit. This led to the creation of a large glass vestibule on the front of the building that allowed people to see its original façade through the glass as well as providing a display space for large items the low ceiling floors in the main museum couldn't allow for. Mechanical and engineering costs were reduced because the existing floors would not be messed around with to the degree originally envisaged.

The excitement was palpable and even though the team knew it would be hard to get the agreement of heritage bodies, they thought the elegant solution offered new opportunities to see the building in its glory and reduce obtrusive works in its interior. Because they were motivated and energised, it was much easier to win over these bodies and the building design and its plans were eventually approved.

The re-emergence of energetic flow in the building team impacted on the museums team who could now work with a clearly defined footprint. They decided to reduce their bandwidth and focus their energy on the design of the displays and in doing so, offered up one of their team who lacked display knowledge. I knew this colleagues skills and potential energy well. Whilst his substantive role was in sales and marketing (to increase visitor numbers and spend), he had a good working knowledge of information technology. I asked him to support the local history team. This proved to be a good 'manager as streamer' move as he made a valuable contribution in sorting out the local history team's online access issues so that they could re-focus on developing the content for the local history service.

In the meantime, I recognised that as the team consisted mainly of people who enjoyed 'digging in the detail' and this translated into a slow, steady energetic pace which was fit for the purpose of cataloguing the vast library of resources the public would want to access. At the right time in the project, I planned to 'increase the flow' of the local history team by shifting them into the future by re-connecting with the sensory landscape view of the service. But for now, there were other priorities and theirs would come to the fore at a future time already identified in the project's sensory landscape.

6   Enquirer

Once the big workplace questions have been asked about mission, vision and values and the processes to deliver them are operating, it is the manager's responsibility to keep on asking pertinent questions in order to refine and renew workplace operations.

Using the 'What Why' process I describe on page 55, the manager fulfils a major part of the role of *Enquirer*. Their role is to ask and find out how people are feeling, what works and what doesn't. This process should be applied to every new project but should also be used periodically as it progresses. Of course, if you ask questions, people will give you answers. The *Enquirer* knows this and will act on them. Instead of reacting to each response, the *Enquirer* will store the responses until a pattern begins to emerge and will then act.

The process of asking questions, listening to replies, storing them until a pattern emerges and then acting upon it, I call 'working the carriage'. Imagine you have to take the same train journey to work at the same time each day. You notice the same work colleagues are also on the journey travelling with you. You can ignore them by reading your newspaper or a book, or you can engage with them and find out how things are. You need to work the carriage daily, in the workplace as if you were journeying together to and from work.

You will recall the story I told you about the central library in Poole as an example of Elastic energy? When we were quite a long way into the refurbishment project, I asked the staff: *'How are you?'* *'What's happening?'* One colleague mentioned a problem she was having at the issue desk and the electronic system used for issuing books, DVD's and CD's. She complained doing the repetitive tasks it made her arm ache. She had the reputation of being a bit of a 'moaner' and I certainly couldn't afford to pay out for a new issuing system. I noted what she'd said and moved on.

As the weeks progressed, a number of other staff confided in me the same thing. One colleague was suffering from repetitive strain injury and two women were under investigation for breast cancer. As the majority of the staff were women in their forties and fifties, the complaints about the issuing system coalesced and they worried about their health. It didn't matter if there was no evidence whatso-ever about negative health effects of electronic issuing systems, the group were *beginning to believe it was true.* This would affect their motivation, commitment and their energy. I'd asked the questions and I'd been given answers. It was up to me to provide a solution.

In the end, I chose to buy a new issuing system and asked my ICT librarian to investigate the (then) new self-issue technology (where members of the public took out their own materials). Although it was not proven technology and too expensive to bring in at the time, I was able to offer a present and future solution that made everyone happy. In fact, with the new issue system in place and our intention to introduce self-issue when the technology was reliable and affordable, it somehow created space where staff were freed up to do outreach work resulting in more people joining the library and taking out more CDs and DVDs. Our income increased and within a year, the new issuing system had paid for itself; an example of Radiant energy being released with a positive outcome I hadn't expected, well worth *working the carriage*!

Other Considerations

I've noticed in workplaces that aren't Energy Intelligent, managers tend to do their work first and manage in the spaces left over. In fact, I've witnessed many managers doing their utmost to 'manage interruptions' for example by closing their door most of the time or by setting meetings in the future that don't help people when they have issues in the moment.

If you practice Energy Intelligent management you will have to get used to *being out of control*. You have no time for your own work; you should attend to everyone else. So, get used to the idea that any professional work you may have takes second place in an Energy Intelligent workplace and if you can delegate what you do in favour of concentrating on and applying the *Six of the Best*, so much the better!

The ENQ manager is in the centre of the action of the group and the reporter of its work, very much 'hands on', giving energy, being energised, giving it back *ad infinitum*. This manager knows how to increase bandwidth and increase or reduce energy flow.

The Energy Intelligent manager is a 'doing' not a 'being'. Managers who do little to practise the *Six of the Best* or live up to their Connector roles are dangerous. If the manager fails to connect with staff, they lose the privilege of supervising others!

Back to the example of Google X: At Google X, "Managers need to keep their staff happy because, Mr. Teller says, 'you don't need your manager's permission to leave a particular section if you believe they are behaving in an obnoxious manner. Not only will you leave but everyone will leave and that guy is going to find himself voted off the island by his own people,' he adds". (52)

....

Now that you have read Chapter eight, it is time to review your skills and activities as an Energy Intelligent Manager and Connector.

Try to answer these questions with a simple Yes or No.

1. I make it my business to find out about my team 'as individual people', their likes, dislikes, interests, skills etc
2. I have regular conversations with my team to ensure they enjoy their work and feel motivated
3. I ensure that my staff have work that enables them to use their skills most effectively
4. I use a range of communication strategies to ensure that I remain fully aware of what is happening among my team
5. I regularly monitor activity to ensure things are going according to plan

6. I appraise my manager of any issues arising and remedial actions that I have taken
7. I ensure my team receive a regular flow of information streams from me
8. I create opportunities for adequate dissemination and cross pollination of ideas within the team
9. I ensure records are kept of managerial interventions and outcomes, available as a learning tool
10. I regularly meet my staff on face-to-face basis
11. I enjoy helping colleagues build relationships and make new connections
12. I ensure mistakes are treated primarily as a learning, rather than a blame experience
13. I respect the priorities agreed within the team's activities
14. I welcome new ideas and innovative solutions
15. I regularly monitor enthusiasm and energy levels within the teams I build
16. I ask searching questions about the work, eliciting creative ideas from my team
17. I value the perceptions my team have regarding their workflow and activities
18. I manage my day to prioritise engagement with my team

So how did you get on?

Whilst it is unlikely that managers will answer Yes to every question, it is important to recognise those questions in which you find yourself feeling resistant or want to answer No, or even 'sometimes', 'occasionally', 'if...' for some questions. This suggests that more consideration should be given to these areas of activity.

For each question that you were *unable* to answer 'yes' to, it is important to consider what support and action you might take.

Writing a personal log specifying situations and circumstances where you feel you might have managed it differently or might have been more effective is likely to be helpful. Learning to ask reflective questions of yourself is especially important. Discussing issues with selected and trustworthy confidantes will also be of benefit, especially if they are able to give you clear, honest and constructive feedback.

It is especially important to raise this for discussion with your manager, in order to be able to agree an appropriate course of action to support your development.

Identifying personal goals and a time-frame for action is important so that you are to take steps to increase your Energy Intelligence as a manager.

Chapter summary

In this chapter we have explored the role of the Energy Intelligent Manager as Connector and considered their function in terms of Six of the Best, Crafter, Sensor, Reporter, Animator, Streamer and Enquirer. A set of questions are provided for you to review your skills and to consider any areas in which you may require additional support, development and practice.

In the next chapter we will consider the principles of Energy Intelligent people.

Energy Intelligent People

Chapter overview

In this chapter you are encouraged to think about the pace of activity in your life. You are asked to note the importance of being aware of the effects that your energy states have on your emotions, to spot whether you are in a healthy, average or unhealthy state, and to consider the costs of using, conserving, wasting and increasing your precious energy levels. It is also shown it is important to consider the effects of gaining false 'highs' in your energy levels and the effect of the outside world on your energy.

In considering the effect of other's energy levels on you the concept of others as 'black holes', 'stars' and 'supernovas' is introduced – watch out for them!

When I think about the world I grew up in as a child in the 1960s and 70s in a market town in Worcestershire, things seemed a lot less complicated and slower than the world I live in today.

On a Saturday, my family would go shopping. There was one supermarket on our high street and it wasn't much bigger than what you would call today, 'a mini-supermarket'. The range and choice of products were limited (mostly tins and packet food), so we'd get our sweets from Woolworth's, our meat from the butcher and our fruit and vegetables from the market. We didn't eat out because apart from the local hotel, there weren't any restaurants. The first Chinese takeaway had recently come to town and the only other alternative for buying food not cooked by 'mum' was the fish and chip shop.

Coffee shops were few and far between and the only type sold was instant or filter with hot milk! No cappuccinos, lattes or machiato's existed in Great Britain then!

We listened to records and a cassette player/radio and taped the Top 40 when it was played on a Sunday night. We watched three television channels in black and white and the news of wars or natural disasters took days to arrive on film. If you wanted to communicate with someone it was via the phone, (we shared a 'party line' with our next door neighbour), post, shortwave radio or telegram.

At school, lessons were taught from books and diagrams drawn on a blackboard in chalk. We used logarithm charts to calculate numbers to decimal points and set-squares and protractors to draw geometric shapes. When I was fourteen, my godmother bought me a pocket calculator, but I could never get it to work.

We drove around in British-made cars that rusted and broke down and on holiday (always in the UK), ate sandwiches in the car and drank tea out of vacuum flasks.

Because we had so little choice in what we ate, drank, spent our work and leisure time, life seemed predictable and certain and we lived it at a steady pace. I recall my energy levels only rose when I engaged in things outside of this routine for example playing sport or spending time outdoors or when there was a family crisis e.g. illness of a relative. Most of the time, our energy levels were on the average of the Energy Spectrum (see Fig 3 on page 35).

Then, one day, we were watching a BBC TV programme called 'Tomorrow's World' and they talked about an invention called the silicon chip and how it was going to change the world we live in.

And boy, how it did!

In less than forty years, our lives have been transformed with the advent of computers, the internet, mobile phones. These technologies focused on making things smaller and more compact for our personal use, whilst the opposite happened in the retail and leisure industries where things got 'scaled up'. Hypermarkets and huge shopping centres appeared on the edge of towns and cheap flights abroad literally opened up the world for travel. This also means people can visit us and with other social and political changes, I've seen and met people from different cultures I'd never known about or imagined I would as a child. Simultaneously, the world seems both a bigger and a smaller place.

In my youth when you wanted something you had to wait for it to come, today it is instantaneous. Emails appear directly on your screen. News and information can be accessed at the touch of a button and our sensory landscape is bombarded by advertising and advice on how we could or should live our lives.

The changes I describe in technology, leisure and demographics over the last thirty years have been nothing short of revolutionary and as we all know, they are happening at such a pace, it's hard to keep up with them.

Thinking about life today, the average family probably has two adults in full time work and two children. They wake up, drive the kids to school, go onto work, collect the kids and take them to evening activities, eat, watch a bit of TV, do housework and the whole thing happens again the following day and at weekends, it's full steam ahead taking the kids on trips and classes, shopping, seeing friends and family and so on. Even though it appears everything is happening at a fast energetic pace, compared to our ancestors (who focused more energy and time on finding shelter and food and working to live) we have significantly more money, time and energy to choose what's important e.g. hobbies, holidays and leisure activities!

Today, nothing seems permanent, everything is quickly changing, things appear unstable and interrupted and also exciting, different, new and accessible.

Energetically, the pace of life has sped up significantly and this is largely due to the speeding up of things in the environment or 'outer world'. I call this *outer spin*. Charles Handy in his paper 'The Age of Unreason' (57) names this 'discontinuous change' (as opposed to the 'continuous change' of my childhood where the future was anticipated as more of the same, getting a little better).

When the world's 'outer spin' was at a slower pace, it was more in balance with my inner world consisting of my beliefs, values, feelings, thoughts, hopes and aspirations. In fact, the 'inner spin' of our internal world has barely changed over centuries. Our human psychology is the same as it was thousands of years ago. Our thoughts take the same energy as they did for our ancestors and our desires (to be warm, safe, loved, to protect our family, to have wealth, to develop and learn) are also not much different. In today's super computer age, we react to things a lot slower than a computer with faster processing speeds 750 million times greater than our own.

The balance between outer and inner spin has become unstable because 'outer spin' is moving much faster than 'inner spin' and anyone attempting to keep the two in equilibrium is going to use up a lot of energy!

Fig 13. Inner/Outer Spin

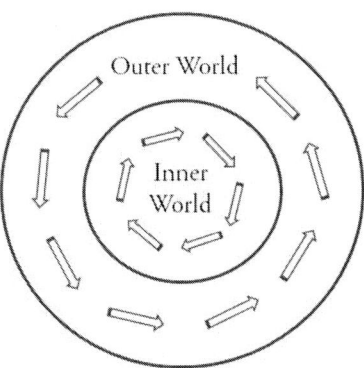

Terms like 'burnout', 'stress' and 'resilience' are in common use signifying the pressure to keep up with the world has a profound impact on individual health and well-being. A publication by an Irish GP, Harry Barry, reflects current thinking and is relevant for anyone living in the modern world: "Irish people caught up in the ever more frantic pace of life are risking both physical and mental health, a GP and author warns....People are placing themselves under high stress and need to look out for early signs of mental health problems.

Increasing workloads, commuting times, housing costs, marital breakdown and alcohol misuse - facilitated in many cases by our increasing prosperity - is an increasing risk to our physical and mental health," he said. (58)

In the Energy Spectrum, the Stress Energy Tensor has been breached and many people are dropping into an unhealthy energy state which *could* become unhealthy and then radioactive. But do they realise what's happening?

"If you put a frog in a pot of cold water and slowly heat it, the frog adapts its body temperature to that of the water until at 100 degrees centigrade it boils alive." Charles Handy uses this story to illustrate the dangers for people who do not notice that the world is changing. People think they are clever at adapting to the changing world; however, according to Charles Handy, people must do more than just adapt to change. "They must jump out of their changing world and take charge of it if they are not to be boiled alive while they sleep."(59)

Energy Intelligent people don't find themselves in a pot of boiling water! They move their focus and energy away from the 'outer spin' and focus on their 'inner spin' by making *energetic choices* about their lives and where and on whom they want to focus their energy.

In the workplace, Energy Intelligent people are aware of the contradictions between the pace of outer and inner worlds. The basic tenet of emotional intelligence is "the ability to monitor one's own and other's emotions, to discriminate among them, and to use the information to guide one's thinking and actions." (60)

The basic tenet of Energy Intelligent People is *the ability to monitor your own energy levels and its impact on others. This requires being attentive towards managing energy in your inner and outer worlds, aware of your energetic relationship with others.*

The Emotional Impact of Energy

To maintain your personal ENQ levels, an understanding of the following will be helpful. Different energy states have an impact on your emotions and your rational acuity.

In my book "360 Wisdom: A Guide to Discovering You"(61), I discuss the impact of healthy, average and unhealthy energy states on our ability to think, feel, be creative and follow our purpose. In relation to our feelings, the following energy states will impact on our emotions accordingly:

Healthy Energy State Emotions (which are at the top of the Energy Spectrum)
- Compassionate, caring, understanding of others feelings.
- Great fun to be around, extrovert, spontaneous, full of ideas, high energy.
- Possessing a great sense of humour that's self-deprecating.
- A quiet and clear mind, calm and confident under pressure.
- Aware and honest about their own feelings.
- Energetic, passionate and open.

Average Energy State Emotions (above the Stress Energy Tensor)

- Trusting of people.
- Generally content and on an even keel.
- Hopeful and confident about the future.
- Can become indecisive and less open to new ideas if busy.
- Slightly fearful if things aren't going to plan.
- Have regret for poor decisions and relationships made and more risk-averse.

Average Energy State Emotions (below the Stress Energy Tensor)

- Tell others how they should be feeling.
- Don't reveal their feelings, internalise them, becoming moody, irritable and self-absorbed.

- Become over-protective of their ideas and get frustrated when they are not taken on.
- Start people-pleasing, putting others' feelings before their own.
- See other people as being controlling.
- Exhibiting anger, jealousy, loneliness if they feel out of control.

Unhealthy Energy State Emotions *(at the bottom of the Energy Spectrum)*

- Rage at what they see as injustice.
- Worry about everything and get lost in the detail.
- Close down their feelings and withdraw.
- Loathe themselves. Lose self-confidence. Feel shame.
- Seek extreme emotional responses from others and will bait them to do so.
- They become locked in by their feelings and can't see a way out of their fantasy world.
- Manifest illnesses for example hypochondria, stress, depression, nervous breakdown.

I have plotted these emotions on the Energy Spectrum in Fig. 14 opposite. The four lightning bolts on the diagram indicate potential trigger points where energy emotions can drop into a lower state. Everyone has a different type of trigger point and it usually comes into play when reminded of a past memory or emotion.

If for example, someone shouted at you at work last month for being untidy and at that time you felt embarrassed and ashamed by the comment, a different person says to you right now: "Your desk is untidy", the brain is likely to process this statement and produce an emotional response of embarrassment and shame *as if it were re-*

sponding to the previous experience, heightening the emotional response to the current episode.

Fig 14. The Energy Spectrum - State of Emotions

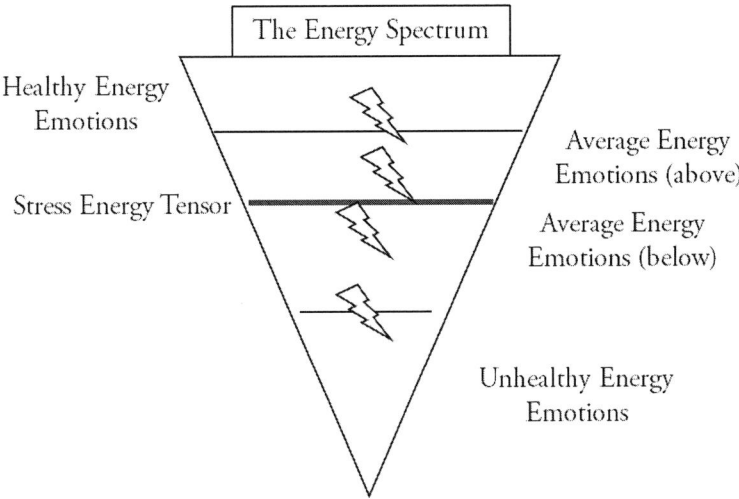

The Energy Spectrum

Healthy Energy Emotions

Stress Energy Tensor

Average Energy Emotions (above)

Average Energy Emotions (below)

Unhealthy Energy Emotions

In the film; 'What the Bleep Do We Know!?' scientist Dean Radin PHD and JZ Knight say: "The brain looks like a thunderstorm-- when it is presenting a coherent thought. So no one is ever seeing the thought. What they do see in Neuro physics is that they see a storm raging around different quadrants of the brain. Those are areas that are mapped in the body and what a person must be responding to-a holographic image-rage, murder, hate...compassion, love.

The brain does not know the difference between what it sees in its environment and what it remembers because the same specific neural nets are then firing. The brain is made up of tiny nerve cells called "neurons". These neurons have tiny branches that reach out and connect to other neurons to form a neural net. Each place where they connect is incubated into a thought or a memory.

Now, the brain builds up all its concepts by the law of associative memory.

For example, ideas, thoughts and feelings are all constructed and interconnected in this neural net and all have a possible relationship with one another.......We build up models of how we see the world outside of us. And the more information that we have, the more we refine our model one way or another.

And what we ultimately do is tell ourselves a story about what the outside world is.

Any information that we process, any information that we take in from the environment is always coloured by the experiences that we've had and an emotional response that we're having to what we're bringing in.

Who is in the driver's seat when we control our emotions or we respond to our emotions? We know physiologically that nerve cells that fire together wire together. If you practise something over and over, those nerve cells have a long-term relationship. If you get angry on a daily basis, if you get frustrated on a daily basis...if you suffer on a daily basis...if you give reason for the victimization in your life...you're rewiring and reintegrating that neural net on a daily basis and that neural net now has a long-term relationship with all those other nerve cells called an "identity".

We also know that nerve cells that don't fire together no longer wire together. They lose their long-term relationship because every time we interrupt the thought process that produces a chemical response in the body-every time we interrupt it, those nerve cells that are connected to each other...start breaking the long-term relationship. When we start interrupting and observing, not by stimulus and response and that automatic reaction, but by observing the effects it takes, then we are no longer the body-mind conscious emotional person, that's responding to its environment as if it is automatic." (62)

Thought-provoking stuff! So, if the brain doesn't recognise the differences in time between one emotion and another and reacts as if these feelings are happening simultaneously, and the brain re-wires itself according to what it practises over and over, it's vital that 'Rest energy' is used to conserve and raise your emotional and mental acuity. By coming off the pace in order to observe what you are thinking and feeling before reacting and repeating the imprinted mental and emotional patterns in your memory, you can choose to act differently with Energy Intelligence.

The Opportunity Cost of Energy

Everything you choose to do uses up energy. If I have a Saturday morning free, I may decide to play tennis. I have to think where I want to hit the ball, hit it, anticipate where my opponent may hit it back and run across the court ready for my next shot. The game will involve my using my mind and body (and probably my emotions if I hit the ball into the net) and I will burn off calories through this physical activity i.e. units of energy originally consumed through eating and drinking.

The opportunity cost is that I could have been using my energy to do something else for example going on a walk, visiting a friend, tidying up my house and whilst there are almost unlimited alternative choices I could have made, *the use of my energy is limited.* I've only got so much of it and when it runs low, I'll need to replenish it.

So, it might be wise to think ahead. If my reserves of energy are limited and precious, where do I want to focus them to best effect? What do I want to achieve when I use my energy?

If it's to have fun, be challenged and stay fit, then play tennis!

In the workplace, we have any number of choices to make about where to put our energy e.g. answering e-mails, attending meetings, writing reports. What most of us do is to try and do a bit of everything, to get the inbox and in-tray down. We often attend meetings when we know that nothing will be resolved and we are going 'for meeting's sake' to show our faces. Think what's really important and make a list of the 'E' (E stands for *energetic)* priorities. Then spend short bursts of energy focusing on each priority until it's completed. When you have fifty tasks ahead of you, it's very de-motivating to work across the tasks and still end up with the same fifty you started with at the beginning of the week. Much better to focus energy on some and complete them and start afresh with a smaller list. Note when I say 'short bursts of energy', I mean spend forty five minutes at a time really focusing on your task, then take a ten minute break. If you work at a desk, leave it and walk around a bit and get a drink and/or possibly a healthy snack. Then resume. This maximises your power of energetic focus and concentration and you will actually get more done.

Waste of Energy

When you think about it, how many things do you do habitually or *because you think you ought to?* There's a close association here with some of the learned values and beliefs you acquired in your childhood and youth which I explained in depth in pages 98. We often do things that are expected of us, or we feel if we don't expend energy on such and such, we will fall behind, miss out on, or not keep up with what's trending. For example, I spend a lot of energy tending my garden, partly because I enjoy it but mainly because I don't want to pay for a gardener. I could probably afford to and re-direct my energy instead into writing books. Even though I know this would be far and above the most productive use of my energy, I come from a family who didn't have a lot of money and consequently we did everything around the house and garden. That said, the garden also helps me stay fit and it's relaxing seeing all the flowers and trees in bloom. So, when I'm making an 'E' choice here, I need to be clear why I'm doing it and what the benefits I get overall.

Similarly, many people spend a lot of energy on social media. Is this energy well spent when the opportunity cost may be doing energising activities with family and friends?

I was listening to a programme on the radio yesterday and the speaker was talking about productivity in work. We are spending a lot of time surfing the net at the cost of getting work done. The key question energy intelligent people should be asking is: "Is this the best use of my energy right now?" Be courageous and stop doing the things that waste your energy. Focus on activities that produce the biggest or best energetic 'E' outcomes for you.

Conserving Energy

This is something I'm finding is more and more important the older I get! Gone are the days where I could stay up all night (and even into the next day) dancing and drinking and talking. The mind and emotions might want to but the body can't quite deliver!

Being self-aware of your energy levels is the first step. Most people know when they have low energy (and many carry on running on low, even empty.) Think about a car running out of fuel. The engine stops because the pistons can't move. Power steering goes and breaking distance increases. Over the years, the petrol tank has gathered sediment at the bottom and this can get pushed into the engine when you try to start it possibly doing harm to your engine and causing the fuel pump to overheat.

The motto here is 'don't run low on gas'. Imagine you are like a petrol tank. Do you feel full, half full or near empty? When you feel your energy dipping and your 'tank' reducing, come off the pace and take a rest. Do what works for you. This may include taking a power nap (closing eyes for ten minutes), having a healthy drink and snack, changing your environment (moving out of your office and sitting in a garden), stretching, doing yoga, Pilates or meditation. Or change your E task (stop typing and read an article for a few minutes instead.)

Increasing Energy

When you recognise you are 'half-empty', this is the time to take action. Your body is telling you it is losing energy and the most efficient way to replenish this is to eat and drink and rest. Often, we get confusing messages. When we feel hungry, we often are actually thirsty. So start off by drinking some water, juice, smoothie or tea.

Many workplaces are air-conditioned and the cold air produced by it is dryer than hot air and you can get even more dehydrated than if you were sweating in a hot and dry atmosphere.

"The dried air pulls moisture from your lungs as you breathe; we can recognize this in a desert condition, but don't think about the effect with cool air. The process of cooling the air causes a great deal of moisture to be lost from it ... ever notice how much an air conditioner drips while it is working?"

The impact of temperature (either too hot, cold or dry) on our energy levels begins "... with impaired mental acuity ... a little slower making quick decisions, forgetting words that you know, transposing terms, errors in work, recreation, sports and everyday activities .... making poor decisions, impaired judgment, stiff aching muscles, headache, irritability .... all before you even feel thirsty ... if your mental processes would let you recognise that you are thirsty. Too often, the fact that you are too busy to think about staying hydrated also causes you to override the thirst reflex. As Ironman Triathlon Champion Scott Tinley said, "You've got to keep thinkin' drinkin'!"(63)

Without going into a long lecture on diet and nutrition, try to eat foods that are low fat and high in protein with some natural sugars and carbohydrates thrown into the mix. Try and cut down on processed foods with high sugar and salt content. Eat and drink slowly and savour every mouthful. Food and drink may be an energetic fuel but it's also there to be enjoyed!

Who says you have to work without a proper break? Don't let other people's unhealthy behaviours affect yours by eating and drinking at your workspace. Treat yourself to a change of scenery for a few minutes.

Learn how to rest when you have low energy. This will relax your mind and body and is a key precursor to being much more creative. (I often take a break when I can't solve something and lie down or walk in the park.) When I come back to work, I often know how to crack it.

There's been a lot of research undertaken about sleep. According to the National Sleep Foundation, "It's a basic necessity of life, as important to our health and well-being as air, food and water. When we sleep well, we wake up feeling refreshed, alert and ready to face daily challenges. When we don't, every part of our lives can suffer. Our jobs, relationships, productivity, health and safety (and that of those around us) are all put at risk. And lack of sleep due to sleep loss or sleep disorders is taking a serious toll."[64] The Sleep Foundation says adults aged over eighteen should have between seven and nine hours of *regular* sleep a night. Setting regular time to go to sleep (the basal sleep need) say between 11pm to 7am is one important factor as is catching up on sleep deficit (this is where you may been sleeping only six hours a night for a month, so you have a sleep deficit of up to thirty one hours). If this is the case, you may have to sleep for longer to catch up on your sleep deficit.

If you find it hard to sleep, don't stimulate yourself by surfing the net or watching television. Do something relaxing like taking a bath or having a massage.

If you eat, drink and sleep well, your mood, attention and energetic performance will be vastly improved

Outer Energy

Over and above the things I mentioned in increasing energy, exposing yourself to the positive benefits of the 'outer spin' in the form of engaging with the natural world will have a beneficial impact. Fresh air, sunlight and regular light exercise provide you with vitamin D and cardiovascular benefits. If you are going to get energised by being outdoors, why not combine it with *walk the dog*?!

"Studies show that when petting a dog, a hormone called oxytocin kicks into high gear. Oxytocin, which is sometimes dubbed "the cuddle hormone," helps reduce blood pressure and decreases levels of cortisol, a hormone related to stress and anxiety.' (65)

Whilst the natural world can provide you with energy, be aware that the 'man-made' world can do so too but at times can be very draining. Ration your doses of the things that you know drain you e.g. watching too much bad news, violent films, computer games on the basis that they can give you a false energy high (see below). I'm not saying that Energy Intelligent people should live a secluded life. Far from it! If Energy Intelligence is about changing the world energetically, you need to engage with it. Some experiences for example computer games provide Rest energy and a bit of escapism, but they can also over-energise. Know when you've devoted enough energy to the thing you are doing.

False Energy

There are lots of stimulants in the other world that give you a false energy high. They include alcohol, drugs, tobacco, sugar and caffeine drinks. They will lift your energy levels temporarily and often can get you through the thing you are focusing on. The after-effects are a bit like the sediment on the bottom of the petrol tank. I'm not going to say 'don't use them' because that's probably unrealistic but use them wisely and for short periods only when you absolutely have to and be aware of their impact on your health and well-being as they are highly addictive.

Energy 'Types'

Your energetic state is going to have an impact on others as theirs will on you. Think about people you work with. When you encounter them individually or in teams do they generally make your energy feel high, average or low? People exhibit a predominant 'type' of energy.

See if you recognise yourself or the people you work with!

Black Holes

I had a work colleague who whenever I met her, I was left feeling drained of energy. I was once part of a team and everything I or another colleague suggested, was met with resistance or indifference. I dreaded these meetings and often left them feeling frustrated and exhausted.

I call people who sap you of energy 'Black Holes'. Black holes exist in space and their gravity pulls in all the energy around them so that even light can't get out. This makes Black Holes almost impossible to see (they are invisible because they don't emit light so you can't see them). In the workplace, there are people who act just like Black Holes. You can only feel the difference they are making to your own energy. You can't see or understand why they do what they do, they are just there doing it!

For years, I tried to understand why people had become black holes in work. Some of the reasons I've already explained in this book. They may not be aware of their values and beliefs and are working in a place that makes them feel uncomfortable. They may be aware of their values and beliefs and are working in a place that doesn't share them. They could be working below their skill level and Potential energy. They may be toxic because they have burned out and don't know how to replenish their energy. They could just be plain bored with life. There could be many reasons or no reasons. They are what they are. I'm not saying you can't help them, but before you do, *help yourself*. You won't be good to anybody if you aren't in an average or healthy energy state and you allow yourself to be pulled down in to their unhealthy zone.

Dealing with Black Holes

The first thing is to not be around them more than is strictly necessary. I've already explained that your energy is precious and there's an opportunity cost every time you use it. So, think of all the positive ways you could use your energy elsewhere before getting involved with a Black Hole.

In work, that avoidance technique might not be so easy. You might have to sit next to a Black Hole or even be managed by one. So, here are some suggestions:

- ✓ Use this as a time for conserving your energy. When you are in the gravitational pull of a Black Hole, imagine you have surrounded yourself with a skin made of Teflon. Any negative energy emitted by the Black hole slides off your skin and can't penetrate it and you can choose how much energy you want to allow through your 'skin' into the outside.
- ✓ Try not to react energetically to anything they say or do. Before you reply or act, *breathe*. Count to ten slowly in your head before you do or say anything.
- ✓ Try to feel compassion (instead of being angry or patronising) for their plight. They must be feeling very toxic and that's a terrible place to be!

✓ Consider whether your energetic response towards them is always the most appropriate. I may be bouncing along like Tigger in the 'Winnie the Pooh' (66) in a high energy state, but should I consider my impact on others? I could be perceived as irritating, insufferable and over-*bearing* (pardon the pun)! If I try to 'mirror' their energy state, perhaps by internalising and conserving my energy more, would that have a positive impact?

✓ Be as relaxed and energetic as you are when you are with people who are in the average energy spectrum or higher. Think about how you are with these people and replicate your energetic response. Notice how the Black Hole reacts and moderate your energy accordingly.

✓ At some point, you are probably going to have to challenge a Black Hole. You can do this by being quietly assertive through asking 'What Why' questions (see page 55). In this way, you keep things objective and focused on energetic outcomes and you never know, in answering the questions you pose, they may reveal the reason behind their energetic state.

Stars

Stars can be grouped together into constellations and are huge luminous spheres of solids, liquids and gases. The nearest star to Earth is the sun and it's the source of our planet's energy. Stars emit energy from their core, radiating into outer space. Astronomers observe stars and can work out its mass by measuring the amount of matter it has and the energy it puts out. The bigger the star's mass, the longer it has existed so in a sense, astronomers can determine its stage of evolution.

In the Energy Intelligent workplace, there are many stars. They have found a 'fit' between their values and beliefs and the organisation they work for. They exhibit healthy energy states and are able to use energy strategies for example Rest energy to observe their outer world and chose how they will respond mentally and emotionally to it.

Stars are lovely people to be around. They are kind, generous and full of ideas and praise. When you work with a Star, it is as if you are the most important person to them because they give you their full attention and are great listeners. Work happens at a brisk pace, but not so active that you can't manage it.

The impact of a Star on your well-being is that you feel full of life and you feel empowered to contribute. Bask in the energy of a Star and absorb their power by mimicking their actions and learning what makes them twinkle!

Stars quite often get 'plucked' out of their role to become managers and ultimately, leaders in an Energy Intelligent organisation, so best be quick or they will be gone someday soon.

Supernovas

A Supernova is the explosion of a star when there is a change to its core (usually caused by it running out of nuclear fuel) and when this happens, some of its mass flows into its centre causing it to collapse resulting in a giant explosion. A supernova burns for a short space of time and distributes its debris into outer space. The debris contains elements and they eventually form new planets and stars.

Be careful with Supernova's. To recognise one, you are going to have to 'feel them out'. A Supernova has all the characteristics of a Star. They are positive, lively, creative, clear-thinking and emotionally intelligent. They appear to be saying and doing all the right things, but you will sense their energy is all wrong. When you observe their body language, they are tense and as taught as piano wire. One sure way of finding out a Supernova is watching their smile. It is fake (body language experts say you can tell this if a person's eyes are not closed, their skin shows no crow's feet, and their bottom teeth are visible). Even though you *should* feel energised around them, you feel uneasy and 'on your guard'. You get a sense that if one thing changes e.g. a push, they may collapse like dominoes or explode.

Supernovas have been very effective Stars and in a workplace that isn't Energy Intelligent, this is often their downfall. The reason? In the past, they have done everything really well and been high energy performers. Managers tend to give them more work because they know they produce results. The Supernova readily accepts more work because they want to prove their worth and meet their own exacting standards. Gradually, the additional workload sits heavier and heavier on their shoulders and they internally show signs of stress. Alternatively, they may have been passed over for key pieces of work, recognition or promotion. They may have fallen behind on a vital bit of training or organisational information, so they are 'out of the loop' and finding it hard to keep up. The precursor to exhibiting the Supernova energy state externally is behaving in a highly-strung and/or frustrated manner and the only way you will pick this up is not by what they say or do but how they make you *feel* energetically to be around them.

An Energy Intelligent workplace recognizes the Supernova desperately needs Rest energy and if you can help them to take 'time out' or practise some of the techniques I describe on page 49 and 50, so much the better. (They will not want to rest because they fear they will fall further behind. Also, sharing your concerns with your manager is important because Energy Intelligent organisations will want to help Supernovas get off the treadmill and become Stars once more, even if it takes a little bit of recuperation time.

Your Energetic Impact

It's worth reflecting whether you are a Star, Black Hole or Supernova and whether you are energetically different according to the people you are with. Do you turn into a Black Hole with some people or become a Star with others? If you can recognise your own energetic state, you can learn to modulate it.

Imagine you are like a tuning fork, but rather than being an acoustic resonator, you are an energetic one. A tuning fork resonates at a constant pitch when it hits a surface and emits a musical tone. Tuning forks have different pitches according to their size. Tune your own 'fork' (yourself) by getting in touch with your own natural 'pitch' by recalling a time when you were in a healthy energetic state. Remember what was happening and how you were feeling and recall your energy levels. Once you have got 'tuned', you can work out whether your present energetic state is at a positive constant pitch or not. If you are out of tune, work out whether your energy level is too high or low and the effect this may have on others. For example, in your low energy state, you may act like a Black Hole and this will de-motivate and drain others around you. In this instance, be honest and tell people how you are feeling and then do something about it! This may involve cancelling your attendance at a meeting if you feel you won't add value or if you can't do this, attend but be very mindful about any contributions you make (you are more likely to see the negative in everything, so before you pipe up with a comment, try to think of a more positive contribution).

When working with people who have unstable energy (they may drop or rise quickly or unevenly along the Energy Spectrum), modulate your energy to theirs so they feel like you are in rapport, and then smoothly bring them to a positive and healthy energy state by listening, asking clarifying questions and co-creating solutions.

Your energy state will impact on everyone you come into contact with and only you can do something about this. It is nobody else's responsibility but your own!

....

Now that you have read Chapter nine, you may find it helpful to answer some questions that will help you be more aware of your own energy levels. Here are 20 to get you started, just try and answer 'Yes' or 'No':

1. I am able to recognise when my energy levels are healthy, average and low
2. I can identify the types of emotions I have when I am feeling 'good' or 'healthy'
3. I can identify the types of emotions I have when I am feeling 'average'
4. I can identify the types of emotions I have when I am feeling low or 'unhealthy'
5. I am able to name the activities that increase and use up my energy levels
6. I can name activities that conserve and waste my energy
7. I am able to pace my day and select activities according to my energy levels
8. I am able to limit the time I spend on activities that decrease and /or waste my energy
9. I am able to extend the time I spend on activities that increase and/or conserve my energy
10. I can monitor the effect my energy levels have on other people

11. I am sensitive to other people's energy levels
12. I recognise when someone is draining my energy
13. I recognise when another person has positive energy levels that suit mine
14. I recognise that I have choices about who I spend time with
15. I recognise that I am currently behaving more as a star / supernova / black hole
16. I choose to eat healthy foods that support my energy levels
17. I am willing to reduce and/or let go of stimulants that give me 'false highs'
18. I know when I need to rest
19. I am able to factor in rest periods during my day
20. I am able to take sufficient sleep to meet my energy needs

How did that go? Although it is a fact in most people's lives that there are times when people, places and things are beyond our control, it is also true that we often have far more choices than we initially believe.

Consider the questions that you were unable to answer Yes – which areas of your life need a little more attention? Work, play, home? People at work, people at home? A particular person? Work-life balance, bed-time? Exercise, diet? Saying yes or no to people? Rethinking how to manage the diary? Rethinking income and expenditure? The list can be endless – the important thing is to think about what really matters to you and try to prioritise. It will not be possible to change everything at once, though changing a few things are likely to make more of a difference than others.

If you feel stuck in certain areas, then think about ways that might help - perhaps writing about it, singing about it, talking aloud, speaking with a trusted confidante, or perhaps coming back to it at a better time when you are less tired...!

Chapter summary

In this chapter we have thought more about our own energy levels. We learn to take note of the things, including people that affect our energy levels. We also come to understand the ways we use up, conserve and replenish our energy. We consider the effect that our energy levels will have on other people and in return, their effects upon us. The questions at the end of the chapter help us to explore this in more detail, and to identify those areas in which we might pay more attention to meeting our own needs.

In the next chapter, we learn more about energy and time and their effects on our energy state.

Energy and Time

Chapter overview

In this chapter I introduce you to the five 'Energetic Time States' and consider their effects on individuals and the Energy Intelligent workplace. These states are: Clock time, Event time, Time Out, Time Surge and Time Fix.

You are encouraged to think of their relative benefits and applications to efficiency and effectiveness in the workplace. Energy Intelligent organisations are aware that time and energy are both precious and finite; they are able to move between the energetic time states, balancing them appropriately with nourishing and refreshing periods of Rest energy. Finally, it is also necessary to consider individual perspectives on time and how this may affect energy levels.

We're busy doin' nothin'
Workin' the whole day through
Tryin' to find lots of things not to do
We're busy goin' nowhere
Isn't it just a crime
We'd like to be unhappy, but
We never do have the time. (67)

Song lyrics by Vaughn Monroe (made famous by singer Bing Crosby)

I recall the time I was in a motorway accident. The car I was driving was doing sixty miles an hour and slowing down as the cars in the distance were stationary. My car was hit from behind because the driver following me wasn't paying attention to what was happening.

As the impact hit, my passenger and I were flung towards the windscreen (thank goodness for safety belts) and assaulted by bags and packages being thrown through the air from the back seats. I expected everything to move in a rush, yet as I fought to keep the car straight, time seemed to slow down and I had what seemed like an eternity to make the decisions needed to keep us safe. Then, time seemed to rush in on me and I made my choice. You could say that in those seconds it took for the crash to occur and for me to park safely on the hard shoulder, I had shifted through different energy time states.

Five Energy Time States

There are five Energy Time States:

Clock Time $\Longrightarrow$ Event Time $\Longrightarrow$ Time Out $\Longrightarrow$ Time Surge $\Longrightarrow$ Time Fix

Fig 15. Energy Time States

1 - Clock Time

We live by the clock, more so than at any point in human history. I can walk into a hotel and behind reception, there may be clocks telling me the time in New York, Hong Kong, Tokyo and Washington. Some of us may have to 'clock into work' by keying a number or swiping a card into a system as we enter and leave for the day. Even if we don't officially clock in or out, the culture of many workplaces is to make Clock Time paramount.

Let me demonstrate how people place importance on Clock Time. When I got my first senior management job, I had a lot of work coming at me and a lot of background reading to do. I decided for my well-being not to take work home in the evenings and at weekends, preferring to stay later and then once home, the remainder of the day was mine to eat, spend time with the family and friends and relax.

So, I stayed in work most nights until at least 7pm. Every time I was locking my door, I noticed all my managers lights were on. For the first couple of weeks I didn't think anything of it. But then I started to realise that they were all working the ten hour days as I was.

One night, I knocked on a colleague's door. "You are working very long hours. Is there a special project you have to complete?" I asked him. He looked sheepish and replied: "Well, you are the boss and you work late, so do we."

In the nicest possible way, I sent him packing and told everyone else that just because I wasn't up to speed and as effective as them, I was staying late to catch up. They didn't need to!

So many of us live our lives by the clock (or by their bosses)! We get up at the same time, go into work and stay until another time when we go home. We eat and sleep at regular intervals and all of this is interspersed by news updates, shop opening and pub closing times.

If we can beat the clock, we love it. We watch quiz shows where people are chased to answer questions in a specific amount of time. When people beat time by running, skiing or swimming faster than the world record in that event, we think it is amazing. We buy products that are time limited on the internet and we dance the night away in clubs that beat the rhythm of clock time.

We have become fixated, even obsessed by clock time and this clock time training takes place from an early age. Our lessons at school are *'time-tabled'* as are lunch breaks, arrival and home time.

The more we watch it and live our lives by it, the more it runs through our fingers. I know several people who live their lives by the clock, their diaries filled daily with appointments. They never have enough time and usually are running late. One person I recently coached was in a manic state where she felt she was *running out of time*. The solution (which seemed totally paradoxical to her) was to take time out, to stop and reassess how she was planning and using her time.

We try to measure time as if it will give us a greater degree of control over it. Not so! Instead it controls us and we are its slaves.

In Clock Time, the focus is on the future, on the activities that are yet to come as well as being aware of the present with a conscious awareness of how much time there is left on any given task or meeting. The stress comes from managing the present knowing a tide of future obligations are coming towards you.

Energy Intelligent workplaces do not operate in clock time. Their mission and vision have set a desired state in the distant future and this operates as an unfolding picture. The future is already there waiting and it won't rush in on you but will come at a measured pace because it has been anticipated in the Sensory Landscape process.

The present 'tense' of being on the clock is not of immediate concern. The Commitment Contract and workplace values place an emphasis on getting the priorities done and trusting employees to do this in the most effective manner. In the ENQ workplace, you are the master of your time and how you use it. As you are Energy Intelligent you will make wise choices about where and how to spend your time and you work in short bursts of high productivity. For ENQ workplaces, the focus is first on *Event Time* and then the remainder of the process to deliver energy time states.

2 - Event Time

"One thing is certain, man has always had a passion for finding better ways to measure it. When it first became important for people to measure time they didn't have or need wristwatches or clocks. All they needed to know is when the winter is coming or when they could plant or harvest their crops. For this the ancient peoples of the earth used the regular cycles of nature. For instance, it was known to them that the sun rises and sets in a regular and predictable way. It was also known that the moons, stars and planets have consistent and predictable motion through the heavens. And they could keep track of the passing of days with sundials and other similar instruments.

With this knowledge they could predict the coming of different seasons..... These early measurements of time were based on the spinning motion of the earth and its rotation around the sun. It is now known today that these motions are not constant but do vary in time." (68)

Event Time means that the focus of activity is in the present and the present is influenced by past cycles. Those ancestors who woke with the dawn and slept just after dusk lived their lives day by day and filled them with activity that needed to be done in the moment. They sensed that the time was right to plant crops or bring in the harvest because in a similar cycle in the past, this had worked effectively. Planting the harvest was an *event*. For those who work in event time, the present is something that naturally unfolds before them and they act almost instinctively on what should be done. Their conscious awareness is on the unfolding of time and not the ticking of a clock.

In reality, we have only shifted substantially from Event Time to Clock Time since the industrial revolution. There are some exceptions. My grandfather whose life was lived in the twentieth century in the countryside, would get up at dawn, live the day by what he sensed needed to be done and would go to bed just after dark.

Even today, some people living on the land are guided more by Event Time, working on their farms from dawn until dusk. I would argue that much of my childhood was spent in Event Time, being immersed in long summer holidays where I lived in the present, playing according to the weather that day and playing with whichever friend turned up in our local park.

Let's go back once again to 'The Heart of the Matter' story. Certain conditions come into play (e.g. the arrival of a suitable transplant). The 'nod' to working in Event Time comes from the CEO and the sense from the team that 'the time is right'. The 'event' is the heart transplant. The work of the team shifts to the present focusing on the job in hand. As they work, what needs to happen next unfolds as each person commences or completes a task. They are focused on results, not time. Ensuring that individuals do their part when needed keeps everyone in the present. Even though there are wider outcomes set in the future, and they may need to 'watch the clock' during the operation, that is not where the focus of attention lies at the beginning of the process.

A close friend has just had a major operation. The consultant told me: "It doesn't matter how long she is under. She won't know about it if I take an hour or two longer. The key thing is that I get it right and the operation is successful."

3 - Time Out

So the heart team ignores Clock Time and moves into Event Time. Then, they reach state three of the Five Energy Time States known as Time Out. You'll recall the line in the Heart of the Matter: *Time seemed to slow to a stop, but paradoxically, they were racing against it.*

By focusing on what needed to be done right then and there, it is as if there's all the time in the world. Seconds seem to elongate so that more energy and action can be packed in. This state of Time Out is similar to the one I experienced in my car crash (when I had in Clock Time only a second or two to make a decision). I found myself being flung into Event Time (the crash is the 'event'.) Then I experienced an expanded sense of the present and moved into Time Out. This gave me an expansive space to work in where I had more than enough time to make a decision.

It is as if for a brief few moments, time had decided to take a break! This is Time Out.

How does Time Out work? If we consider Fig 10 (shown on page 145) once again, rapid bursts of energy from people applying Superfocus powers of observation in the present creates a hyper-surface of present time.

When an individual or a team direct their energy and concentration on an activity or event so that gives 'Superfocus' (if they are observing) or Hyperfocus (if they are working in and on the task), their consciousness about time shifts from a two dimensional into a three dimensional space. What is created is an expanded hyper-surface of the present and it has a large surface area as you will see in Fig 10. Below is another way of looking at the hyper-surface of the present.

Fig 16. Two and three dimensional time states

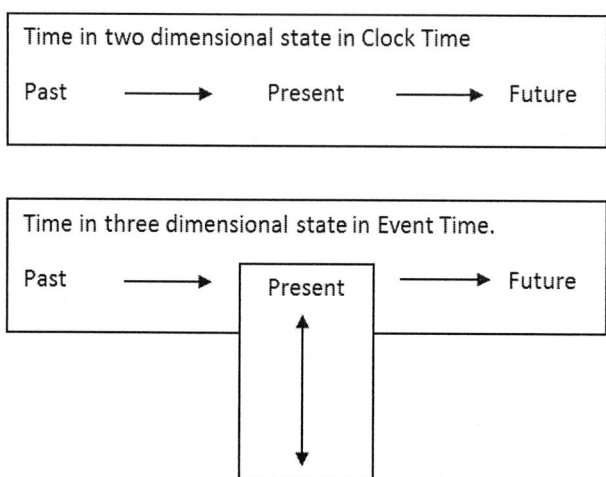

In effect, this is an added depth to time. It's no longer just horizontal (in two dimensional space moving from past to present to future), but has vertical depth in the present making it stretch out longer. In the hyper-surface of event time, the present expands, creating Time Out.

In our awareness of time, time doesn't have a flow outside of our consciousness and only our consciousness gives it a linear meaning. As most workplaces are not Energy Intelligent, they lack a three dimensional consciousness of time, operating along the two dimensional line of 'clock time' awareness.

People working with Energy Intelligence are consciously aware which time state they are working in. This is because whether in a state of Super or Hyperfocus in Event Time, the actions they undertake are happening sub-consciously. This may seem paradoxical, so let me explain.

The surgical team work at a sub-conscious level. They are so highly proficient at what they do, they are no longer conscious of the tasks they perform. They are in Stage Four of Abraham Maslow's Four Stages of Learning (69) (see below), right at the pinnacle point of the triangle.

Fig 17. Abraham Maslow 4 Stage of Learning

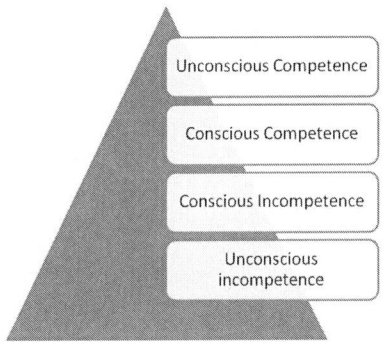

In the hyper-surface of the present, the surgical teams work quickly and efficiently in a state of unconscious competence, yet if you asked them to describe how time worked for them, they would say that their pace was easy and relaxed as if time stood still and they had as much of it as they needed.

Recall a past event or project at work when you believe you were off Clock Time, in Event Time and in this three dimensional state of *Time Out.* Describe how time worked for you in relation to your energy levels and what you were able to achieve. I bet you stopped clock watching and lost track of time and were surprised how much time had passed. When I'm writing, hours can pass by and I don't notice. It feels like I've been sitting at my computer for a few minutes. I've got all the time in the world. Here, I can also get a lot done in a short space of time (like I did in my car crash when time became elongated whilst I chose what to do, yet in clock time, only seconds had passed). We are very conscious of our energy levels in Clock Time and can feel depleted or energised according to how we are feeling about the task we do. In Event Time, the awareness of our energy levels becomes unconscious and it becomes a natural flow. If we shift into Time Out, it is as if we are able to tap into an energy source beyond that found in our physical being; something far more universal and of unlimited power.

When the task is completed and we return to Clock Time, only then do we become aware of our physical energy levels and our conscious notion of time.

When this happens, we are often amazed at how much Clock Time has passed. In deep levels of concentration (the heart transplant teams did their work over a period of hours), this becomes apparent when they finally stop working and notice it has gone dark! Whilst they have been working, Clock Time flies. When I do anything that takes a great degree of concentration e.g. skiing down a black run or windsurfing or writing a training programme or a report, I focus on the 'event' and move on into *Time Out*. I do this by committing myself completely to the task (I reframe it as an 'Event') in hand and that means no distractions of any kind until it is completed. For many people, this could be an issue. It's hard to keep concentration on one thing and very easy to be distracted by the internet, social media, the phone call to a friend not yet made, cleaning, cooking etc. Unless you make this kind of effort to get into Event Time, the clock will rule you and your energetic response.

The difference between my client who was manically living by Clock Time and the surgical teams, is that they made a *conscious decision* to come off Clock Time to focus on Event Time knowing and trusting that it would lead to a sense of time out where everything they needed to do would be completed. The washing of dishes, making of beds and eating food could wait!

"Albert Einstein was sitting in his chair at the Patent Office in Bern one day when the breakthrough happened." Suddenly, the thought struck me: if a man falls freely, he does not feel his own weight. I was taken aback. This simple thought experiment made a deep impression on me," he wrote in 1907. This was two years after the publication of his Special Theory of Relativity and it led directly to his theory of gravity, and still later to his General Theory of Relativity. In effect, Einstein had stumbled upon one of his greatest insights: gravity is acceleration.

From this simple concept came the idea that the stronger the gravitational pull on a clock, whether it is from a planet or another massive object, the slower time itself would run. It would mean, he predicted, that time would run faster and people would age more quickly the higher they were from the ground.

Einstein said that realising gravity and acceleration were the same thing was "the happiest thought of my life". It is at the heart of the theory of relativity, which states that time and space are not as immutable and fixed as we think they are from the immediate experience of everyday life.

With the invention of atomic clocks, which can now measure time to billionths of a second and are accurate to within one second over 3.7 billion years, scientists are now able to show the truth of Einstein's predictions about how time can slow down or speed up depending on the position and speed of whoever is making the observation." (70)

So, if an experience in everyday life is an 'extra-ordinary' event and it takes a greater degree of focus, energy and concentration, then time is not as fixed as we think. Time can slow down or speed up according to our state of consciousness.

---

4 - Time Surge

When the task that took our Super or Hyperfocus to complete it is finished, we drop from Maslow's unconscious competence learning state down to an incompetent conscious state. All of a sudden, we become aware of Clock Time once more; of other commitments made and meetings to attend.

Simultaneously, energy time states shift backwards. The Time Out and Event Time states move back into the default state of Clock Time. This happens as a *Time Surge*. (This is the time I have to be most careful as I shift back into Clock Time. It's much more likely when I revert to doing something mundane e.g. doing the cooking or washing up, that I'm likely to burn or drop something). If you've ever been close to blacking out but have managed to stay conscious, you will know what I mean! The Time Surge can literally knock me off balance. It is as if I whoosh back into a different reality!

I recall that after I'd managed to take control of my car by driving it onto the hard shoulder, it was as if time that had stood still rushed back into my consciousness with a multitude of thoughts and feelings. Cars were honking, a policeman arrived and opened my car door. I breathed and felt shaky and aware I'd almost been killed. I looked at my watch and realised I was going to be late getting to my parents for dinner and that I'd have to ring work to tell them what had happened. Time Surge brings the minutiae and the mundane of Clock Time ticking back into our consciousness.

Time Surge occurs at the point when Super or Hyperfocus on an activity or event is removed. Usually, this happens when the activity or action is completed, our energy is dissipated and we lose Super or Hyperfocus. Thus, we slip out of Event Time and back into Clock Time.

5 - Time Fix

Energy Intelligent workplaces and people can control the shift along the time states to Time Out by creating a suitable 'event' that reignites the interest and motivation levels of staff as soon as the Rest energy and reflection period is over. This event should be time-defined e.g. it will be completed in a day, a week, a month or a year. When I announced the refurbishment of the central library would be completed within a year, I was aware I would need to create a series of events and related activities that would give a present 'Hyperfocus' where Time Out would be created to complete them and enable ordinary work and duties to carry on too.

A project lasting a year? That must be too long for people living in Clock Time to cope with? The flow of time is much longer than we are aware of in Clock Time. You just need to get your head around it! If we employed a longer time perspective and didn't worry that the important changes take time, we'd be much better at moving along the energy time states. If we think of our country and some of the issues that need sorting e.g. long term unemployment, changing the economic base or improving education and health, they will certainly take far longer than the elected term of a politician and a government. Indeed, some of the problems we face we've been having for decades if not centuries!

To deliver a big change needs careful planning (Sensory Landscape, IDEALS and What Why processes) plus an understanding of the timeline needed to deliver it. It also needs to be seen by the workplace as a ground breaking 'event' to be delivered with a series of mini 'events' set periodically along the timeline to aid progression. Then, good leadership and management should encourage people to 'take time out' from Clock Time activities to concentrate on the event when the time is right!

Energy Intelligent workplaces can manage the time states and are capable of thinking many years ahead despite the pressures to live in the present in Clock Time. One amazing experience I had of 'long time thinking' was doing some planning for a team running a cathedral. These days, the church operates like a business. This cathedral had 200 staff, 600 volunteers and a turnover of £28 million.

We were looking at their strategic plan. The vision was: "In 3018, the cathedral...." I thought there must be a typing error! Yet, they were thinking a thousand years ahead to a time, after everyone sitting around the table, their children and great grandchildren would be long gone. Yet, the 'institution' had been around for 2,000 years and their cathedral for over a thousand, so why not Time Fix on a grand scale a thousand years into the future?

In a sense, the cathedral's leadership team manages time as if they are Time Lords (see page 157). They observe the flow of time and as the future unfolds (e.g. the stained glass in a rose window decays over time and reaches the point where it needs repairing), they move into Event time and *act.* They repair the stained glass and it takes as long as it takes. It's an important event in the timeline of the cathedral. Time Out then occurs until the task is completed. Then, they experience a Time Surge and they move back into Clock Time to consider their next project or activity. The whole process may happen over a week (or in the case of repairing a large stained glass window, months or even years.)

Taking Rest energy to properly reflect on the completed 'event' also provides Time Out. This enables colleagues to not only replenish their energy levels, but to expand their awareness of the hypersurface of the present. Having a team conversation about how everyone's awareness of time and its impact on their energy during the 'event' will lead to profound insights and bonding which will give a heightened state of awareness and confidence for planning and experiencing the next 'event'. It will also refine the use of the Five Energies e.g. when to use Elastic Energy and when to 'kick back' as Kinetic Energy builds its own momentum.

When the team are conscious that what they do in the expanded present will have effects into the near future, this can create a Time Surge. However, in this instance, the surge is both *anticipated and managed.* Unlike my car crash (where I was placed in an unknown situation and couldn't predict what would come rushing at me on the hard shoulder e.g. more cars, the police, breakdown trucks, the driver who'd crashed into me), Energy Intelligent workplaces anticipate the Time Surge. This is because they have an understanding of the business that will rush in on them from the future through the Sensory Landscape process. They have already worked backwards in time from their future workplace vision with all its iterations, projects, programmes and actions needed through to the present. All

225

they have to do now is to choose where to place their focus of attention. The super position of multiple possibilities about all the things they could be doing, collapse into one event. This becomes the activity they *fix their time upon*, and in doing so, enter the last stage of the time states; *Time Fix*. The activity is completed and fixed in time and exists in the memories of the people involved in its creation as well as the people who will use it, change it or replace it in the times to come through the workplace Learning Library.

The Opportunity Cost of Time

However we mark or measure time, or how we choose to consciously operate within it, all time is precious because it is ultimately limited in our Newtonian, deterministic world. If we choose to focus on one event over another, the opportunity cost of our time is the thing we chose not to do. Workplaces often don't make the time to develop the events to choose from, nor consequently can they choose one thing above another. Instead, without these priorities (or in some workplaces I've visited, everything is a priority!), they spend a bit of time on everything and wonder why nothing is ever completed.

ENQ workplaces are clear about the finite nature of time and energy and have developed sophisticated ways of prioritising what's important. They apportion their precious time accordingly by thinking about the impact the activity will have in Time Fix. Once they are committed to using this time on this activity, they never waste a second in instigating it and using every drop of time in a targeted way. After all, time is money, so it's said!

Individual Time Perspectives

In their remarkable book 'The Time Paradox', Philip Zimbardo and John Boyd (71), show how we have an individual perspective of time and it shapes how we interact with the world.

They put forward six time perspectives for the Western world, two past, two present and two future:

- **Past-negative:** People who view the past as a negative experience because it was. Sometimes, they reconstruct harmless past events making them more negative than they originally were. They live in the present replaying what happened, wishing they had done things differently. They hope they can avoid the pain they've endured in the future and don't do much to change their anxious state by changing their mind of their circumstances.

- **Past-positive:** These are people who have a positive view of the past (either through positive memories and beliefs and/or through making the best out of difficult situations that occurred.) The past influences their present thoughts, feelings, beliefs and behaviours. They like continuity and convention and are confident, friendly and fit well into society.

- **Present-fatalistic:** 'What will be will be' is the motto for this time perspective. Present-fatalistics don't believe anything they do will change their life. They believe they have been given 'their lot in life' and it makes them apathetic, down and dull. Their fatalistic sense of 'it doesn't matter what I do' means they will consume food, drink, drugs aware of the possible consequences but not caring because they are already 'doomed'.

- **Present-hedonistic:** They engage in anything that makes them feel good in the 'now'. They like adventure, good times and are spontaneous. They don't worry about the future, how they will live. Money is spent not saved and they will eat and drink whatever they like, not worrying about the consequences to their future health.

- **Future:** These people plan ahead, set goals and are high performers. They are prepared to forego pleasures in the present for a greater reward in the future. They save for a rainy day and watch what they consume. When the rainy day comes, they continue to save and never use what they have. Life ends and it hasn't been lived!

- **Transcendental-future:** They believe that life is just one stage of a more profound process. These people believe in life after death and have a deep religious or spiritual practice. They have good control over their desires, are in control of their life and are aware of the future consequences of their actions.

My explanation of each time perspective is only cursory and I strongly recommend you read Zimbardo's excellent book to understand the time perspectives and how to manage them in more detail.

What is interesting, is how individual time perspectives impact on Energy Intelligence. For example, a workplace with a preponderance of present-hedonists would provide great bursts of energy on existing activities and events and would probably get quickly into Event Time and Time Out. They would have little care of the company mission and vision or a sense of their impact on the future or for future consequences. They wouldn't relate to a workplace interested in anything beyond the short-term e.g. Time Fix and planning longer-term events. They would consume resources and devote far too much time, without regard to the opportunity cost.

Present-fatalistics and Past-negatives would be focused on Clock Time looking at their watches and thinking how slowly time passed. They would find difficulty concentrating on the event, and possibly find it boring or distracting or even pointless. Energy levels would be low because they wouldn't believe anything they did would have a positive impact or because they remembered when things had been tried like this before, they had always ended badly. The past-positives would provide a counter-balance by reminding these types that it might be worth giving things a try, but they would take a limited view of the future and be risk averse to try something new or different if it hadn't got a root or pattern they could associate with the past. They would be great at being in Event Time because it would remind them of how their ancestors lived, but would be slow to react to Time Surge and Time Fix to focus on an unfolding event from the future.

The future perspectives type is in many ways more suited to the concept of Energy Intelligence and the energy time states. It chimes with their spiritual sense of time flow. They would be great at contributing to mission and vision and the sensory landscape process but less capable of managing their conscious states within the energy time states. Future types already find it hard to live in Clock and Event Time and would not see the point of placing their Hyperfocus in a present event. They would rather plan ahead and remind everyone of the approaching time surge and what event or activity 'coming round the corner' should be time fixed.

Zimbardo and Boyd indicate their 'Ideal Time Perspective' through a process of heightening the positives and removing the negatives.

They suggest the optimal time perspective is:

- High in past-positive time perspective
- Moderately high in future time perspective
- Moderately high in present-hedonistic time perspective
- Low in past-negative time perspective
- Low in present-fatalistic time perspective

" This blend gives you roots....connects you to yourself across time and place...provides a sense of continuity and allows you to be connected to family, tradition and your cultural inheritance....(*past types*)..You can envision a future filled with hope, optimism and power...to soar to new destinations....to escape the status-quo...(*future types*)...gives you energy and joy about being alive. This energy drives you to explore people, places and self...it is life-affirming (*present types*)." (71)

The ideal time perspective above describes both a person with a high state of Energy Intelligence with the ability to work along energy time states efficiently and effectively. Time and energy become synchronised and the ideal time perspective type uses them to optimum effect.

ENQ workplaces should be mindful of the time types they recruit to their organisation as it will have a significant impact on their ability to function. Perhaps as part of the selection processes, potential employees should take the Zimbardo Time Perspective Inventory (see http://www.thetimeparadox.com/zimbardo-time-perspective-inventory/) so that employer and employees don't waste each other's time!

....

Now that you have read Chapter ten, here are some Energy Questions to consider:

1. Do you recognise these time states within your own life? Make some notes about them and think about when and how they have occurred. What features do you recognise?
2. Do you recognise any of these time states within the workplace? Describe features that you recognise.
3. Within the workplace is there a flow between states?
4. Might you/the organisation do more to help the time flow?
5. Using Zimbardo's descriptions, where do you fit? Can you recognise the fit with other colleagues? What ideas come to mind here?

Chapter summary

In this chapter we have explored the range of energetic time states and their relevance to the workplace. We have also considered individual perspectives on time and how this may affect energy levels. Ideally, an Energy Intelligent workplace will be mindful of recruitment and will have colleagues who have both a high appreciation of energy states and an ability to work across a range of energy time states.

In the final chapter, we review the key messages of Energy Intelligence.

Review of Energy Intelligence

I'm hoping that by the time you reach this part of the book, you will have a greater understanding of the Energy Intelligence theory and the ways in which you, your colleagues and your workplace can become more ENQ. By now, you will know that Energy Intelligence is a way of operating in work that is an holistic approach that whilst it has constituent parts, they are all inter-related and inter-connected. You cannot take the 'm' out of $E = MCC$ for example!

The Sum of the Parts

So, if I wanted to extract some key points for you to take away with you to apply, it's hard to do. If you've ever tried to build a house of cards and managed to use all fifty two of the pack to create an edifice, if I came along and pulled half a dozen cards from different parts of the structure, you would de-stabilise it and the whole lot would fall down.

So, I'm mindful to not say one part of Energy Intelligence is more critical than another. They are all equally important if you want to build a stable 'house' in your workplace.

Measuring the effects of ENQ

One of the things I am aware of that we haven't done (beyond asking you a set of questions at the end of each chapter) is to suggest a measurement system for E = MCC. Most workplaces will want to see a rate or return for their investment in ENQ. This can take many forms e.g. improved performance, increased profits/surpluses, reduced customer complaints, improved market share.

Every workplace will have a different idea of measuring success according to their vision, mission and values and business plan. So I don't want to suggest a 'one size fits all approach'.

Some of the questions you've been asked throughout this book could form the basis of a system that quantifies the effectiveness and efficiency of past actions completed under Energy Intelligence. I also suggest you start by revisiting your employee engagement processes. Most workplaces offer some kind of staff survey. You could consider creating a series of qualitative questions around whether individuals feel personally engaged with the workplace, with their teams and their manager. You could track this year on year to see whether improvements are being made. To dig deeper into the data, I recommend an 'engaged space' that takes place just after staff survey results are in. This could take the form of a series of focus groups representative of a cross-section of the workforce. Handled sensitively, you would be able to get some rich information about where to make changes to improve the energy of your place.

The above process combined with team meetings, one to one's and staff appraisals would give you feedback on any issues around motivation and commitment and of course, the Commitment Contract and its underlying processes is designed to help here as well.

For quantitative results, you could also reinterpret other performance data that most workplaces collect. For example, an ENQ workplace should see reduced sickness absence year on year. Drilling further into the detail, you could expect to see less workplace stress and related health conditions e.g. mental health, improved blood pressure, sleep patterns.

You should also expect higher staff retention rates and more job applicants citing they want to work for you because of a 'fit' between your values and theirs.

Another fascinating area you could consider for verifying the impact of Energy Intelligence will be your impact on customers and the wider environment. Measurements of improvement could include:

- Higher customer satisfaction ratings
- More 'likes' on social media
- More followers on social media
- Reduced customer complaints
- More customer praise
- Positive media coverage

Tailor-making an Energy Intelligent performance measurement system is something we can advise you on together with ways in which you can make your workplace ENQ so you can be at the forefront of rapid change and reap its opportunities.

Patience!

I've found that if I want to change the way I am, the way I interact with others and how to improve the way I work, it takes energy, time and patience. Energy Intelligence won't offer you a 'quick fix' like so many management and personal development theories claim they do. Like diet fads, you may try them for a few weeks, even months and see some change, but is it sustainable? You lose weight and then gradually, over time, you put it all back on (and possibly a bit more...)!

Energy Intelligence is a radical new way of looking at how to make your workplace fit for purpose to cope with the rapid change we are experiencing in our globalised and complicated world. If you commit to wanting to be ENQ, you will need to devote time, energy and resources to seeing it through. But the effort will be worth it and the rewards will outweigh any costs. For who wouldn't want to work in a place full of happy, committed, resilient and high-performing employees, where you give excellent customer-service and have built a reputation in the community far beyond your reach?

If I gave you one piece of advice, it would be to say that the change starts with YOU. That may sound a bit 'motherhood and apple pie', but the reality is that unless you want to change and effect change in yourself to take on board the basic tenets of Energy Intelligence, you won't do a damn thing to make it different for anyone else.

So, once you understand the basics of $E = MCC$, focus on aspects of the book that relate to you personally. Everyone should read Chapter 9 Energy intelligent People and if you are a manager or leader, read those chapters (8 &7) that relate to you specifically. If you can:

• Recognise your energy levels in yourself and others.
• Know how to replenish your energy.
• Know when to energise and when to rest.
• Understand how and when to energise the people around you and when not to.
• Keep away from falling into black holes!

- Understand how precious time is and know how to use it wisely,

......then you stand a good chance of being able to help other people in your workplace to become ENQ.

It's a big 'if' I know, but as the poet Rudyard Kipling in his great poem 'If' said:

"If you can fill the unforgiving minute
With sixty seconds' worth of distance run,
Yours is the Earth and everything that's in it," [72]

And that has to be worth trying for.....?

Epilogue

Right now, workplaces stand at the centre of two paradigms with one foot in each model. Paradigm one is what I call the 'Separate', and it originates from the Renaissance or classical period where people began to see themselves and be considered as individuals, viewing the world from a subjective perspective.

Since then, the notion of individualism has gradually separated humans from nature, from their community, collective and ultimately from a sense of society.

The 'Separate' paradigm translates everything outside the self into discreet operating parts that are related if only the links or gaps between them can be found and understood (also known as the mechanistic view). Clock time measures this separation. Science, management science and the arts developed into individual disciplines to reflect this perspective.

Because we have traditionally tried to see the whole through the parts, it's not surprising if we cannot understand the flow of energy and time and our relationship to the natural world. We are also unable to see the effects of the interactions we make to discreet areas. We tinker in one part and it can create fault lines elsewhere. So, whilst we continue to do this, global warming and the recent credit crunch and anything else that may arise, will always be an unpredictable surprise.

We are also struggling with the notion of leadership. We don't respect our politicians, bankers, doctors and teachers like we used to and in some cases, they have done little to earn our respect. Perhaps we are a little harsh? Leadership is hard work! Leading workplaces in a fragmented world is so complex it's almost beyond the capability of one individual. Anybody who wants to step onto the final rung of the leadership ladder chooses to do so with trepidation for the job may give big rewards but it also brings great pressure and stress. (If you don't believe me, look at how badly Presidents and Prime Ministers age!)

In the workplace, the rapid pace of change means structures and management systems are wobbling and jobs are no longer 'for life', creating mental, emotional and physical instability for many people.

The old adage 'better the Devil you know' is still being played out. Despite all the inherent problems arising in our maintenance of a world view that is no longer fit for purpose, we tend to stick with what we know. Here are some of the positive and negative characteristics of the Separate Paradigm on the workplace. (I'll leave it to your judgment to decide which is which!)

- Buffeted by rapid change
- Singular, discreet businesses in competition with others
- Management theory offers a plethora of solutions with few predictable results
- Mechanical view of workplace systems operating 'like clockwork'
- Only exists if seen, tested, measured and empirically proven
- *Most* things are predictable and evolve from past patterns
- Economic success a motivator
- Individualism is foremost

- Big is beautiful
- Someone has to be in charge
- Hierarchical structures
- Provides stable processes and systems

In a world of globalisation, rapid change, developments in new technology, the rise in wealth of second and third world countries, the Separate Paradigm seems an anachronism, yet there's nothing obvious to replace it with. Yet, if we look to *what lies underneath*, there is hope and possibility.

Theoretical physicist David Bohm said: "The notion of a separate organism is clearly an abstraction, as is also its boundary. Underlying all this is unbroken wholeness even though our civilization has developed in such a way as to strongly emphasize the separation into parts."(73)

In his book *One from Many: Visa and the Rise of the Chaordic Organization*, Dee Hock the creator of Visa asks the question: "What if the very concept of *separability* (mind/body-cause/effect-making/nature-competition/cooperation-public/private-man/woman-you/me) is a grand delusion of Western civilization, epitomized by the industrial age; useful in certain scientific ways of knowing but fundamentally flawed with respect to understanding and wisdom? What if our notions of separability, particularity, and measurement, useful as they may be in certain circumstances, are just momentary, mental aberrations in the mysterious evolution of consciousness?"(74)

There is a sense that something new and different is emerging. Paradigm two, the 'Unified Whole' emerged from twentieth century attempts in science and the arts to break the mental and physical barriers between disciplines, by attempting to join them together in different combinations. The evolution of science to the point of discovering the quantum world has found a reality that our mechanistic, rational view of the world finds hard to comprehend.

Yet, even though the procedures, standards and laws are often contradictory to those of the tangible world, the quantum environment is beginning to affect our notion of physical reality. Here are some of the positive and negative characteristics of the Unified Whole paradigm as viewed through the quantum world.

- Can hardly be seen. Operates on a very small scale.
- Challenges conventional wisdom e.g. objects can exist in multiple states and places at *the same time*
- Rife with uncertainty and riddled with paradoxes
- Separate from objective reality
- Can create conditions to produce huge amounts of energy
- Works on a different notions of matter, time and space
- Augments present reality
- Places an upper limit of knowledge (the Uncertainty Principle states you can never know the position and momentum of a quantum object)
- Connected in the sense that quantum objects are linked or entangled because changing one affects the other at a distance
- The whole and connectedness is the thing, yet the 'Holy Grail' has not been found (the attempt to describe all fundamental forces and the relationship between elementary particles in a 'Unified Theory').
- Yet, even without the theory, there is a sense that there is a Unified field made up of abstract potential, being, consciousness, ideas, concepts and information.

"One is led to a new notion of unbroken wholeness which denies the classical idea of analysability of the world into separately and existing parts ... We have reversed the usual classical notion that the independent 'elementary parts' of the world are the fundamental reality, and that the various systems are merely particular contingent forms and arrangements of these parts. Rather, we say that inseparable quantum interconnectedness of the whole universe is the fundamental reality, and that relatively independent behaving parts are merely particular and contingent forms within this whole." (75)

For now, the scales are tipped towards the Separate, but as we discover more about the quantum world and how its discoveries can be applied in everyday life, they will become balanced and then who knows what may develop!

Already, inventions emanating from the quantum world are having an impact on our daily lives. The laser, transistor, the electron microscope, magnetic resonance imaging have helped to make transformational leaps in computing, medicine, chemistry and the arts (lighting effects at the 2012 London Olympics would never have been possible for example).

Energy Intelligence at Work was written to provide a bridge between the Separate and the Unified Whole. Looking into the future, I want to 'tease' you with some of the possibilities beyond the scope of this book (but maybe will be captured in the next) that are emerging from the Unified Whole paradigm.

The Observer

We will all need to develop the role of Observer beyond my description in the Energy Intelligent leader and the Energy Intelligent time states. There is still a great debate in physics about the role of the observer in experiments. Physicists Albert Einstein and Niels Bohr profoundly disagreed about this. Bohr believed the act of measuring something had a profound effect on the reality of things and the observer would play a role in this.

According to Bohr, in any experiment, the act of measurement makes the outcome real and substantive and someone or something operated by someone has to do the measuring. Einstein insisted that objects must have physical attributes that are always actual and real, quite independently of any observer or act of measurement.

Today, the Bohr view, where the observer is as an active part of the process is accepted, mainly because Einstein was never able to prove that there was an underlying natural order that unified the classical and the quantum world. Einstein was convinced there was and one day a Unified Field Theory would be found, leaving him to lament: "As I have said so many times, God doesn't play dice with the world." (76)

Today, in Wave Particle Theory for example, the wave becomes a wave or a particle depending on the observer. If we aren't witnessing waves and particles, we don't know which they are! If we can 'pop' or collapse the quantum wave function by observing matter at a fundamental level and having it emerge in the form we choose, what can we 'pop' or collapse in the material world? If we can learn to hone our observer skills to a fine degree, what could be possible? We could change the properties of so many material things and our conscious perception of reality.

The leader as observer already has a major role to play in Energy Intelligence, but I suspect that improving observer skills across the workplace will become more important in the future and may well reveal a new physical level of operating.

The Thinker

The notion of the Separate has even developed into celebrating the separation of brain function. Historically, the mechanistic view celebrated 'left-brain' thinking. The ability to analyse, use logic and to process is still regarded by many as being more important than being 'right brained' (using intuition, imagination and creativity). In reality, it's a bit more complex than this. The healthy brain is not as dichotomous as was previously thought. The best results are produced when both halves of the brain are working. We need both divergent and convergent thinking using our intuition to sense something and then apply deductive reasoning to understand a problem and solve it. Einstein possessed both divergent and convergent thinking skills in equal measure for he imagined and visualised travelling along a beam of light before applying rational thinking to what this might mean.

In order to train ourselves to be more brain balanced, we need to 'tune up' our right brain so that we can consciously apply what we sense, intuit and imagine. This will involve serious consideration on how we educate young people in the coming years and help adults to 'unlearn' the over-use of the left brain.

(If you have little concept of the right brain function, watch the amazing Jill Bolte-Taylor discussing what happened to her when she had a stroke and found herself 'existing' completely in her right brain as a stroke affected her left brain function see: http://www.ted.com/talks/jill_bolte_taylor_s_powerful_stroke_of_insight).

In the coming years, new ideas will augment our present notion of reality and a new reality will form. As we collectively create that new reality, we will only see it when we step out of it, *observe* the changes and *think* about them. We may well cease to exist in Clock Time and operate backwards in time (from the point of Time Fix) managing time as a series of events and enjoying surfing Time Surges when they come!

When we see how much our routines and behaviours have altered, our memory and our future thinking will become encoded with a new 'synaptic' structure. We will learn to break habits and make different choices and changes and learn the art of 'plasticity' both within brain function and in our ability to re-shape our material world. Perhaps we will see our brains more as a laboratory where we play and learn to experiment because there will be many events and experiences that come that will fall outside our existing notions of reality?

For example, scientists have already demonstrated when two people are placed in separate Faraday cages and one is asked to think of the other, the receiver has an awareness of when the thinker is thinking of them. When evidence is emerging to show subconscious entanglement between people's minds, there is much to consider about the energy and power of thought both inside the self and its connection to others outside of the self and the implications for accessing the quantum world 'at will'.

The Unified Field

In quantum mechanics, Zero-point energy is the energy that remains when all other energy is removed from a system. In the zero-point field, everything is connected. Scientists are finding that in this 'empty space' there is a sea of light and there is unbelievable energy and this could be a vital source for us to use in the future. I am certain that new sources of energy will be discovered in the coming century from the Quantum world, transforming the way we live, work, and understand life. It will take Energy Intelligence onto the next level.

New Workplace Forms

"A healthy organisation is not a collection of detached human resources who simply look after their own turf. It is a community of responsible human beings who care about the entire system and its long-term survival." (77)

As workplaces apply and use E=MCC, there will be a greater degree of trust and unity between people and this will be evaluated and understood by a higher level of performance measurement. They will create new forms of qualitative and quantitative measurements to assess the impact of E=MCC using variables that relate to their sector, industry and wider environment.

ENQ workplaces of the future will be much more adaptive and egalitarian. Think of the hive or the termite nest and how they operate in nature. Both adapt to their environment and work in synchronicity with it and each other. Everyone has their role and important function and it is both separate and inter-connected. There may be the equivalent of a 'Queen Bee' or a termite King and Queen in the workplace. In the hive, it is to procreate and once offspring emerge, to leave and then once their task is completed, others take over and play their crucial part e.g. feeding, repairing, producing. Leadership of a high ENQ functioning workplace could be metaphorically similar with each person having a vital and specific role to play to ensure the survival and prosperity of the workplace.

ENQ workplaces will have much looser structures, less hierarchical organisational forms and be connected by alliances, shared aims and outcomes. Knowledge will be stored and shared widely with everyone. Workplaces will be thinking, feeling, creating and believing systems.

Time

In the Unified World, we will understand time in a very different way and manage its flow accordingly. In the quantum world, time can go backwards (back in time to where the information was unified and then it goes forward once more.) This is the theory of the Big Bang and cosmologists and astronomers are already working backwards in time by measuring light energy emitting from stars to understand our universe from the beginning of time. Workplaces will become adept in using and recording time moving forward, back, up, down and along timelines. Time will be understood and viewed more subjectively as individuals get to grips with their own time perspectives and how they relate them to work.

We will be far more relaxed about time and will build space into our working day to allow time to *unfold*.

Communion

In writing this book and remembering what living in the past was like (before the internet age, mass consumerism and the globalised world), I can see the changes and how they have affected me.

I recognise I am no longer the person I was and nor is the world the place it once was. In order to really grasp what this means, I've had to 'die a little', to surrender to the changes and let go of the past. Whilst it's important to bring elements of the past into the present to keep a sense of identity and stability, we need less of the past to guide us than we realise.

The death of the old self and the old workplace is painful and costly but if you are prepared to enter into this journey of self-acceptance, I believe it is the only course of action. I suppose what I'm advocating for some will be 'borderline insanity' because much of the empirical evidence your left brain will tell you to be on the lookout for, won't be there!

But as the 'new self' and 'new workplace' emerges and the old patterns and ways of doing things tumble, a new horizon of experiences and opportunities that bear no resemblance to anything you've ever known or experienced, will emerge.

Spiral Dynamics is a dynamic model of human development based on the 1970's theories of psychologist Clare Graves introduced in the 1996 book *Spiral Dynamics* by Don Beck and Chris Cowan. (78) They argue that human nature isn't fixed and we can adapt to new environmental conditions by developing new conceptual models. The 'Spiral' is a system of core values or collective intelligences applicable to individuals, groups and cultures. Each level in the spiral represents a level of human existence. The higher levels in the spiral are dependent on the lower levels. If one level were to be removed, all the levels above would collapse. So, in contemplating a shift to a higher level of consciousness it can only be one that takes with it all the lower levels. The higher levels are dependent on the lower levels, not the other way round.

At the upper end of the spiral is the level turquoise. Turquoise thinking uses the entire spiral in an integrated, holistic way, understanding how each stage in the evolution of the spiral is essential and necessary for the health of the whole. Qualities of the level turquoise include:

- Experiential learning
- Uniting feelings with knowledge
- Transpersonal living
- Refreshed awareness of energetic fields
- Ability to detect harmonics and pervasive flow states in organisations
- Sensing waves of integrative energies
- Working with a collective consciousness (multiple levels interwoven into one conscious system)
- Universal order not based on external rules or group bonds

"To operate consciously at turquoise, one begins to understand one's own evolution to date through the various developmental and cultural layers in one's own life; to perceive and understand this in others; and to get a grasp of the direction of one's evolutionary trajectory." (79)

Energy Intelligence has been written to do exactly this. It is a journey about our own evolution, in understanding how life has developed and changed culturally for each and every one of us and the impact this has had on how we work. It hopes to show a glimpse of not just where we have evolved from, but a route we might travel in the future.

At turquoise, a theory of everything is possible in theory and actuality. Whilst Einstein died without ever finding his Unified Theory,

Energy Intelligence offers a contribution towards something more harmonious; an integrated model that may bring together leaders, managers and staff to collectively and holistically tackle some of the challenges they will find just waiting around the corner.

If Energy Intelligence has raised your consciousness onto the next level, my work is complete for now.

There is still much to learn but the journey is no longer about going round in circles, it's about moving up a spiral staircase!

1. https://www.goodreads.com/author/show/1140617.Nikolai_Lo bachevsky (see p12)
2. Heart of the Matter by Amanda Beech BA CMIPD http://www.learning2xl.com/about_us/about_l2xl.htm (see p20)
3. Interview with Mihaly Csikszentmihalyi, Geirland, John (1996). "Go With The Flow". *Wired* magazine, September, Issue 4.09. (see p32)
4. Walter Isaacson, The Real Leadership Lessons of Steve Jobs, Harvard Business Review. http://hbr.org/2012/04/the-real-leadership-lessons-of-steve-jobs/ (see p33)
5. Peter Drucker. Thoughts on Leadership. Forbes. http://www.forbes.com/2004/11/19/cz_rk_1119drucker.html (see p37)
6. Geshe Michael Roach. The Diamond Cutter: The Buddha on Managing Your Business and Your Life p 169. Doubleday, 2003. (see p48)
7. Core Index Database. Simplyhealth Group http://www.coreindex.co.uk/company-profile.php? companyid=7869 (see p48)
8. Top 20 Most Awesome Company Offices by Josh Dunlop. Income Diary.http://www.incomediary.com/top-20-most-awesome-company-offices (see p49)
9. BBC World Service. http://www.bbc.co.uk/worldservice /sci_tech/highlights/010104_milliebug.shtml (see p53)
10. Arthur Murphy. 'Don't get blinkered: involve end-users to ensure IT projects stay on road to success'. Computer Weekly. http://www.computerweekly.com/feature/Dont-get-blinkered-

involve-end-users-to-ensure-IT-projects-stay-on-road-to-success (see p57)

11. Pralahad & Hamel 3:5:3 Strategic Fit and Strategic Stretch Strategy MBA Book 1 Introduction p25 Open University B820 Book 1, 1996. (see p64)

12. Professor Paul Burns. Extract from: Corporate Entrepreneurship: Building the Entrepreneurial Organization (2nd Edition), Paul Burns, Palgrave Macmillan, 2008, http://www.palgrave.com/uploadedFiles/Richard%20Branson%20and%20Virgin.pdf (see p65)

13. Understanding Evolution. http://evolution.berkeley.edu/evolibrary/article/history_14 (see p68)

14. Charles Handy. The Age of Unreason. Chapter 20, Creative Management edited by Jane Henry. The Open University, Sage Publications 1996. (see p68)

15. David Muir, 'the Power of Brands'. http://www.wpp.com/~/media/sharedwpp/newsletter/thestore/documents/thestore_newsletter_006_thepowerofbrands.pdf (see p69)

16. Heather Stewart, Economics Editor the Observer, 'This is how we let the credit crunch happen, Ma'am ...' Sunday 26 July 2009 http://www.theguardian.com/uk/2009/jul/26/monarchy-credit-crunch (see p70)

17. NuYu http://nuyu-ksa.com/ (see p76)

18. Google mission statement. www.google.com/about/company (see p77)

19. Coca Cola vision and mission statements. http://www.coca-colacompany.com/our-company/mission-vision-values (see p78)

20. BBC mission, vision and values. http://www.bbc.co.uk/aboutthebbc/insidethebbc/whoweare/mission_and_values/ (see p78)

21. Oxfam. http://www.oxfam.org/en/about/what/purpose-and-beliefs (see p78)
22. NHS England vision and purpose. https://www.england.nhs.uk/about/our-vision-and-purpose/ (see p80)
23. NHS Core principles. http://www.nhs.uk/NHSEngland/thenhs/about/Pages/nhscoreprinciples.aspx (see p80)
24. REEL Cinemas. http://www.reelcinemas.co.uk/ (see p85)
25. Abraham Maslow. http://en.wikipedia.org/wiki/Abraham_Maslow (see p89)
26. Intrinsic and extrinsic motivation. http://en.wikipedia.org/wiki/Motivation (see p90)
27. Victor Vroom Expectancy Theory. http://www.learnmanagement2.com/vroom.htm (see p90)
28. UK Median Weekly Pay, Datablog, Guardian Newspapers 12.12.2013. http://www.theguardian.com/news/datablog/2013/dec/12/uk-median-weekly-pay-is-517-but-who-earns-that (see p90)
29. What is Self-Determination Theory? About.com Psychology. http://psychology.about.com/od/motivation/f/self-determination-theory.htm (see p91)
30. Forbes Magazine. http://www.forbes.com/sites/jeannemeister/2012/06/07/corporate-social-responsibility-a-lever-for-employee-attraction-engagement/ (see p93)
31. The Guardian. http://www.theguardian.com/sustainable-business/responsibility-good-business-long-term (see p93)
32. Aristotle. http://classics.mit.edu/Aristotle/rhetoric.3.iii.html (see p94)
33. Massey. http://en.wikipedia.org/wiki/Morris_Massey (see p99)
34. Florida. http://www.theatlanticcities.com/jobs-and-economy/2011/12/diversity-leads-to-economic-growth/687/ (see p109)

35. Caffè Nero http://www.caffenero.com/story/Ethics.aspx (see p111)
36. Steve Pavlina. http://www.stevepavlina.com/blog /2011/10/what-is-commitment/ (see p116)
37. Hippocratic Oath. http://news.bbc.co.uk/1/hi/7654432.stm (see p119)
38. Caryl Rusbult. http://www.carylrusbult.com/(see p120)
39. Peter Drucker. Thoughts on Leadership. Forbes. http://www.forbes.com/2004/11/19/cz_rk_1119drucker.html (see p134)
40. In the Black-for strategic business leaders. http://www.itbdigital.com/opinion/2013/11/05/how-do-you-make-the-leap-from-cfo-to-ceo/ (see p137)
41. Dale Carnegie 'How to Win Friends and Influence People'. Pocket Books 2010 (see p140)
42. Glassdoor. http://www.forbes.com/sites/ jacquelynsmith/2013/11/13/how-to-show-appreciation-and-get-better-results-from-your-employees-this-holiday-season/ (see p140)
43. Aesop. http://www.storyarts.org/library/aesops/stories/boy.html (see p143)
44. Peter Senge & C Otto Scharmer & Joseph Jaworsky & Betty Sue Flowers: Presence Nicholas Brealey, 2005 (see p146)
45. Nova, Michio Kaku. http://www.pbs.org/wgbh/nova/ physics/theory-behind-equation.html (see p148)
46. Alice in Wonderland, http://www-history.mcs.st-and.ac.uk/Quotations/Dodgson.html (see p149)
47. Lynda Gratton, Glow. P159. Prentice Hall, 2009. (see p150)
48. Vanessa Able. http://www.theguardian.com /commentisfree/2014/feb/03/tata-nano-car-cheap-poor-safety-rating (see p150)

49. Dr. Edward de Bono. https://en.wikipedia.org/wiki
    /Po_(lateral_thinking) (see p151)
50. BBC News Pay-per-minute café opens. 15 January 2014
    http://www.bbc.co.uk/news/magazine-25733143 (see p152)
51. Anita Roddick. http://www.thebodyshop.co.uk
    /services/aboutus_anita-roddick.aspx (see p152)
52. Secret Google lab 'rewards staff for failure' By David Grossman
    http://www.bbc.co.uk/news/technology-25880738 (see p153)
53. Time Lords. https://en.wikipedia.org/wiki/Time_Lord (see
    p158)
54. Henry Mintzberg. Managing Prentice Hall, 2009 (see p165)
55. Winston Churchill. http://quotivee.com/2013/articles/quote-
    explained-winston-churchill-success/#sthash.lPrt7BCJ.dpuf
    (see p173)
56. Csikszentmihalyi, M. (1998). Finding Flow: The Psychology of
    Engagement with Everyday Life. Basic Books. (see p173)
57. Charles Handy 'The Age of Unreason' Chapter 20. Creative
    Management Edited by Jane Henry, Sage Publications 1996.
    (see p188)
58. Harry Barry. Hectic pace of life causing mental illness Posted:
    Wed 04/04/2007 http://www.irishhealth.com
    /article.html?id=11279 (see p189)
59. Charles Handy, The Future of Work in a Changing World
    Interview by Maxim Jean-Louis. http://aurora.icaap.org
    /index.php/aurora/article/view/52/65 (see p190)
60. Salovey & Mayer, 1990 http://www.unh.edu
    /emotional_intelligence/EIAssets/EmotionalIntelligenceProper/
    EI1990%20Emotional%20Intelligence.pdf (see p190)
61. Claire Chidley, '360 WISDOM: a Guide to Discovering You.'
    Gatehouse Press 2011. (see p191)

62. What the bleep do we know. http://www.script-o-rama.com/movie_scripts/w/what-the-bleep-do-we-know-script.html (see p195)

63. Scot Tinley. http://www.klemmerhead.com/vitalyte/hydration-101/science-articles/causes-of-dehydration/ (see p199)

64. Sleep Foundation. http://sleepfoundation.org/article/how-sleep-works/how-much-sleep-do-we-really-need (see p200)

65. USA Today. 'How Dogs Spread Happiness'. http://yourlife.usatoday.com/parenting-family/pets/story/2012-01-24/How-dogs-spread-happiness/52756792/1 (see p201)

66. A.A. Milne http://www.amazon.co.uk/Winnie-Pooh-Complete-Collection-Stories/dp/0416199615/ref=tag_stp_s2_edpp_url (see p204)

67. Vaughn Monroe. http://songmeanings.com/songs/view/35308221078590766221/ (see p211)

68. Temporal Measurement Dr. David Lewis Anderson http://www.andersoninstitute.com/temporal-measurement.htm (see p215)

69. Maslow's Four Stages of Learning jasongregory.biz (see p219)

70. Indpendent. http://www.independent.co.uk/news/science/einsteins-theory-is-proved--and-it-is-bad-news-if-you-own-a-penthouse-2088195.html (see p222)

71. The Time Paradox, Zimbardo and Boyd. Rider 2010 (see p227 and p230 my italics)

72. IF by Rudyard Kipling http://www.poemhunter.com/poem/if/ (see p237)

73. David Bohm, The Undivided Universe. http://www.goodreads.com/work/quotes/197918-the-undivided-universe (see p240)

74. One From Many: VISA and the Rise of the Chaordic Organization, Dee Hock P4 Berrett-Koehler Publications, 2005 (see p241)

75. David Bohm. On the Intuitive Understanding of Nonlocality as Implied by Quantum Theory, Foundations of Physics, vol 5, 1975 (see p243)
76. 1943 Einstein in conversation with William Hermann's book Einstein and the Poet, P58 (see p244)
77. Henry Mintzberg: Managing Prentice Hall, 2009 p223 (Watson 1999) Co-operating in communities. (see p247)
78. Spiral Dynamics, D. Beck & C. Cowan. Blackwell Publishers, 1996 (see p249)
79. Conscious Embodiment by Michael Wolff http://www.academia.edu/4010688/Conscious_Embodiment1 (see p250)

[Please note: All internet links referenced in the above Bibliography were last accessed on 1 February 2016]

ILLUSTRATIONS

INDEX

Claire Chidley MBA, MA.

Claire is an experienced trainer, facilitator, coach and public speaker. Her company Create Tomorrow Today has been designing and running leadership development programmes, training for managers executive coaching and conference facilitation for local authorities, national parks, housing associations and corporates. She is a SOL-ACE (Society of Local Government Chief Executives) Associate Trainer and leadership consultant and a Fellow of the Royal Society of Arts.

Prior to her current role, Claire worked as a Partner in Comedia advising world cities on cultural regeneration programmes and she had a 20 year local government career, latterly as a Corporate Director in Test Valley Borough Council in Hampshire until 2007.

Claire is a published author and international speaker and has worked in the USA, Far East, Middle East and Europe. She is an expert in developing organisational values and critical thinking techniques to improve organisational performance and motivation. Claire is passionate about encouraging and developing personal responsibility in order to improve team working and problem-solving. Her facilitation style is inspiring, engaging and open. She believes people learn best when they are having fun and are energised! So, she wrote 'Energy Intelligence at Work' to help you get the most out of employees in terms of their motivation, commitment and energy.

See www.clairechidley.com

Claire is supported by **Dr Julie Baldry Currens** who has used her extensive experience as a senior manager in the health and higher education sectors to enrich the ideas behind 'Energy Intelligence at Work.' Julie has more than thirty years of education and training experience, gained in the NHS and Higher Education sectors. Her knowledge and skills help individuals and organisations grow, learn, change and realise their full potential. She has a national and international reputation for her work, with particular expertise in the field of workplace, practice-based and collaborative learning.

For consultancy and development, Julie combines expertise in education with sound practical experience, gained through senior roles as Clinical Specialist, Head of Leadership and Strategy at the Higher Education Academy and Director of Learning and Teaching at the University of East London. She specialises in training and advice in a range of activities including leadership and professional development, people, team and resource management and programme design, implementation and evaluation.

Julie advises and assesses universities and other private/public organisations. She currently holds advisory roles in Great Britain and Australia; she is regularly invited as a conference /workshop speaker and trainer. She has worked in Great Britain, Ireland, Sweden, Italy, Saudi Arabia, Malaysia and Canada.

The quality of Julie's work as educator, academic, trainer and developer has been recognised by her peers- she is a Principal Fellow of the Higher Education Academy and has been awarded the highly prestigious and internationally recognised National Teaching Fellowship Award for excellence in learning and teaching.

See www.higher-ideas.london